MICKEY MANTLE
Is Going to Heaven

MICKEY MANTLE
Is Going to Heaven

FRITZ PETERSON

Outskirts Press, Inc.
Denver, Colorado

Outskirts Press, Inc.
http://www.outskirtspress.com

ISBN PB: 978-1-4327-4384-0
ISBN HB: 978-1-4327-4673-5

Library of Congress Control Number: 2009930696

Outskirts Press and the "OP" logo are trademarks belonging to Outskirts Press, Inc.

PRINTED IN THE UNITED STATES OF AMERICA

Contents

Acknowledgements

I appreciate my wife of over 35 years for letting me have time to write this book expressing my thoughts concerning my feelings toward my living and deceased teammates, fellow athletes, and writers, wherever they may be.

Thank you Bob Evely, a minister of a Church in Wilmore, Kentucky, for the constant help in keeping the spiritual part of this book in line with what the Bible teaches and for helping me with the unusual, one of a kind, glossary. Although some of my comments concerning the 1,000 year millennial baseball game between the Yankees and the Mets are, or course, imagined, the rest of the book is quite serious. Mr. Evely has a M. Divinity Degree from Asbury Theological Seminary and was ordained in the United Methodist and the Free Methodist denominations. Thanks for keeping me on track where it counted.

Talking about "on track", thank you Jim Roth, our faithful attorney for going through all my statements in an attempt to keep me a free man in this litigious society. Glad you're a Yankee fan!

Thanks to Dr. Richard Williams, University of Iowa Clinic, for keeping me alive long enough to finish this project. I appreciate the research project you helped me get into in an effort to slow the progress of my recurring prostate cancer.

Thanks to you too, Byron (and Anita) Tobias for your editing. I'm sure you had to look twice several times at the content in a few of the chapters concerning what really went on inside the clubhouses I inhabited over the years. What I wrote did happen. Good luck in your writing career!

Thanks to some of the greatest Yankee fans of all times for reviewing these chapters and adding their thoughts. Dick McCauley, former ABC Radio Vice President, Danny Austin, Ph.D., Professor Emeritus, Nova Southeastern University in Ft. Lauderdale, FL, and Susan J. Fescharek, a lifelong Yankee fan and personal friend, for a woman's perspective.

Thank you Mrs. Thelma Smith (wonderful mother and wife of 3 of my "Yankee Fantasy Campers") for her insistence on me doing this book "my way", as different as that might be.

Also thanks to Marty Appel, ex-Public Relations Man for the New York Yankees and ongoing, successful author of many sports books, for straightening out some of my forgotten baseball facts. Good luck on your book, "Munson—The Life & Death of a Yankee Captain"!

For the families of the deceased players I wrote about, and the ones who are still on this earth. Remember: the thoughts I presented in this book are only my opinion. God is the final judge and He never gives up. There's still time to be added to the "active roster" if you're not on it yet. Anyway, after the last out is made, everything's going to be OK!

I Miss Mickey!

(When asked if he thought Mickey Mantle was going to Heaven,
former teammate and a pallbearer at Mickey's funeral, Johnny
Blanchard said, "Where Mickey's going, it's HOT,
I can guarantee you that!" 11/22/06)

Bobby Richardson came to the mound in my very first inning pitching for the New York Yankees during our first road series of the 1966 season and said, "Do you hear what Mickey is yelling"? I said "no" (I was concentrating on the hitter, Frank Robinson, the number 3 hitter for the Baltimore Orioles and didn't hear "anything"). Bobby told me Mickey was saying "hurry up"! The reason Bobby came in to tell me this is that he didn't want me to take it personally, especially in my first game in the big leagues. What Mickey was trying to tell me, in essence, was that it wasn't necessary for me to take my time between every pitch just because I was in the big leagues now. I now know that players, especially outfielders, like to keep a game going at a faster pace since the time goes by slower for them because they aren't involved in every play like the infielders are, especially with sinkerball pitchers like me or Mel Stottlemyre on the mound.

Ever since that time, I became one of the "quickest" pitchers in the league, once completing a game in an hour and 18 minutes in a nine inning match against Ferguson Jenkins later on in my career. The media loved it too since they could get their stories in to their papers sooner so they could get out to the bars and restaurants quicker after games, especially on road trips. The writers and I thank Mickey for that! One time a writer even asked me why I worked so quickly out on the mound. I answered (honestly), "So I can hurry up and see who wins". They loved it and I really did too! Thanks Mickey!

The first time I personally saw Mickey was in 1963. I had been invited to work out for the Yankee "brass" while the Yankees were in Chicago for a road trip in June of that year. I had just come off of a career making season at the college I ended up graduating from, Northern Illinois University, earning all kinds of honors in Division One College baseball in the season that just ended.

I got to ride on the team bus from the hotel in Chicago, where I had just eaten breakfast with my dad and 2 of the Yankee scouts, to the ballpark for my tryout. It was a thrill to be on the same bus and hear the Yankees chatting and joking on the 15 minute trip to Comiskey Park. I was amazed to see that I was taller than Mickey Mantle, Roger Maris, and especially Whitey Ford. I was only 6 feet tall. But I noted Mickey's forearms. As big as Popeye's! Guys look so much bigger on TV!

The next time I would see, and actually meet Mickey, was 2 ½ years later in spring training of 1966. I had been placed on the 40 man roster and was invited to spring training with the big club after a really great season the year before, splitting the season between Greensboro, NC (A ball) and Columbus, GA. (AA ball).

Mickey was awesome! He knew rookies were reluctant to come up to him and say hello because he was so incredibly famous. So he would actually come over to us when the occasion presented itself and say, "Hi, I'm Mickey Mantle". As if we didn't know! That's how he was in the clubhouse.

Mickey liked me even though I wasn't in his "group" per se. He was at the twilight of his career (in pain) and I was just starting mine.

His buddies were mostly gone by that time, Billy Martin, Yogi Berra, John Blanchard, etc., but Whitey Ford was still there even though Whitey was almost beneath his twilight with severe circulation problems in his pitching arm. All in all, Mickey wasn't having much fun by the time I got to the Yankees.

I nicknamed Mickey "Thumper", which he liked. It came from a game in spring training in which he hit a monster homer (right-handed) off of a hard throwing left-handed pitcher for the White Sox by the name of Juan Pizzaro. Other than a homer that Boog Powell hit off of me in 1970, the one Mantle hit off Pizzaro was the hardest shot I ever saw. Because of that, I nicknamed him "Thumper". I wish I could have been there to see some of the tape measure shots he hit in his prime!

One night, on a road trip to Baltimore in 1967, Mickey and I ended up in the same restaurant after a game. Whitey was a coach at the time and didn't stay out as long as Mickey that night so Mickey ended up by himself at the bar. When it came time for the restaurant to close I saw Mickey leaving by himself and looking a little tipsy. I decided to walk him back to the hotel because it wasn't a real good part of town and I didn't want to see him get hit by a car, or maybe mugged.

On the walk to the hotel Mickey gave me some good advice. He said, "Hey Fritz, if you ever see someone driving toward you with a hand over one of his eyes, get off the road, it's me, and I'm drunk! I do it so I don't see double!" I thanked him for the advice as we laughed and went to our rooms in the hotel.

By 1968, Mickey was the only one left from the most recent Yankee "dynasty" days. Stottlemyre, Pepitone and Tresh were still there but they had come in after the real core of the Yankee team that had been in place before their arrival. Really, Mickey was the only one that virtually everyone wanted to see. I remember thinking, how can anyone go watch the Mets across town, a "no name" team when they could still come to Yankee Stadium and see a living legend, Mickey Mantle, play. They did, however as Yankee attendance was down to an all time low from the last 20 years while at the same time the Mets continued to draw fans from a city that had been abandoned by the Dodgers and the Giants less than a decade before.

As much as I couldn't stand the Mets or their fans, their team was really beginning to put something together. They did it mainly with pitching. They had Seaver and Koosman and a few other excellent pitchers but they were still only the Mets, a no name team from nowhere! The Yankees were (and are and always will be), the Yankees and still had #7, Mickey Mantle on their active roster!

Many times I saw Mickey hounded by autograph seekers, especially after the last game of a home stand when we would take a bus from Yankee Stadium to LaGuardia Field in the Queens for a road series. Fans would swarm the players for autographs when they came from the clubhouse to the bus, especially Mickey. Most of the time Mickey would sign 40 or 50 autographs until the bus driver had to close the doors to pull away from the curb. Some of the remaining fans would yell obscenities at Mickey for not signing their items. I still haven't figured out what "Schultz'" means but many times he would get "You Schultz"! Mickey was a nice guy but I could tell things in the "big apple" were getting to him. Along with the pain in his legs and the Yankees not winning anymore year after year and with little hope of improvement in the near future, the party was coming to an end for Mickey.

Fans would still try anything to get Mickey's autograph. When I first came up, the other rookies and I would be targeted by seasoned fans trying to get to Mickey. Very often they would say to us, hey, tell Mickey his high school coach was up here (in the stands) and would like to say hi to him. I, like the others, would fall for it a few times but Mickey would never embarrass us but instead would let us figure it out for ourselves. Once in a while, just to pimp an untruthful fan, Mickey would actually come over and sign his ball or whatever with "Best f---ing wishes, Mickey Mantle". I hope those people kept those autographs since those were real, most others weren't!

Each day of a home stand the first thing most of us would do was head to the table in the middle of the clubhouse to sign baseballs. Usually there were about 4 dozen baseballs sitting on the table to be autographed. When we were through we would get our uniforms on and head out to the field to take batting practice and get loose for the game. Mickey would come in a little later than the rest of us but his name was already signed on the baseballs, on the sweet spot, an isolated place on the baseball where there was only room for one autograph, a spot quietly reserved for the "star" of the team who, of course, was Mickey.

A few times after games Mickey would leave before me and the next day I would beat him to the park. After a while I realized that Mickey didn't sign those balls on the table at all—our clubhouse man, Pete Sheehy had done the "honors" for Mickey. Needless to say, thousands of people have gotten signed Yankee baseballs with 24 authentic signatures on them and one fake one, the fake being the only one that really counted. Mickey's!

Big Pete was very secretive. He had been there since Babe Ruth and knew things about all of us that he would never ever tell anyone, thank goodness. He could have written dozens of books about what he knew and learned in the clubhouse over the years but it was a known fact, you could trust Big Pete. Just think of how we might feel if Big Pete had told what he knew about Lou Gehrig? The name of the movie, "The Pride of the Yankees" might have to be changed!

I was there when Mickey hit the homerun off of Denny McClain on September 19, 1968 in Detroit. I also pitched a game that year against McClain in Detroit, though not the one Mantle hit his 535th in. Denny was unbeatable that year!

I overheard Mickey say in our clubhouse the night I faced McClain, "Who's the lamb tonight for us", meaning; who would be getting tonight's loss for our team because we were facing McClain. Mickey didn't know I was in the clubhouse getting my pregame stretch, but I was to be the "lamb". I never told him I heard it because he would have felt terrible.

McClain, who should have been left-handed the way he behaved, was somewhat crazy. Fun-crazy in a way. He had done some dumb stuff like pouring a bucket of ice water on the head of a wonderful older Detroit newspaperman, Waddy Spoelostra, but on September 19, 1968 he did something really nice for Mickey.

Denny sensed that Mantle would not be back to Tiger Stadium again because of his age and physical problems (knees mainly) so when Mickey came up to bat later in the game with Detroit leading by 3 or 4 runs he called his catcher, Bill Freehan out to the mound and told him that he was going to "groove one" for Mick. McClain told Freehan to ask Mickey where he wanted the pitch to be. Freehan did it and I remember seeing Mickey put his hand out about waist high and over the middle of the plate to show McClain where to throw it. McClain did it but Mickey just took the pitch for a strike! Mickey didn't believe he'd do it! McClain did it again and Mickey fouled it back. But the third time he connected for #535. Mickey would only hit one more home run, the next day in New York, but unless I had seen it with my own eyes, I wouldn't have believed what had just happened with that pitch to Mantle in Detroit that night!

The homer was both a very happy occasion and a sad one at the same time. Happy, of course, because Mickey hit another home run but sad because he "almost" needed help to hit a home run at the end of his fantastic career. I'm glad that he didn't need any help the next day against Jim Lonborg at Yankee Stadium where he had hit so many before, especially when they counted. It was truly an honor to have played with him as my teammate for 3 years and to have been the starting pitcher for the Yankees on the day that he hit his last major league homerun. I wish our time together as Yankees could have been longer but he was in so much pain at the end that I was actually relieved for him when he decided to retire! If he had known how hard it would be to earn money right after that, he might have decided to play longer despite the pain. Babe Ruth found out the same thing.

While Mickey was angry that he didn't end up a career .300 hitter (.298), another great player who flirted with a career .300 mark was Al Kaline, the toughest hitter I had to face over my entire career in the big leagues. Kaline was having a horrible year (for him) in 1973. It was actually sad to see Al struggle even though he had given me a lot of trouble during Yankee/Tiger games for years. He was a real thinker at the plate and a real competitor. He was still trying to find a way to beat you if it were the 8th inning and his team was trailing by 8 runs.

The Tigers were in New York for a series in 1973 and Kaline was at the point, in the game that I was pitching, that he needed one base hit to bring his career average up to .300. Having seen what Denny McClain did for Mantle in 1968, I had our catcher, for that game, Duke Sims, a former teammate of Kaline's the year before, come out to the mound to talk over the situation concerning Al's average. Duke told me earlier that day that if Kaline got a hit the Tigers were going to take him out of the game immediately and Kaline would retire as a lifetime .300 hitter.

Kaline was good at everything so Duke suggested that he would tell Al to lay a bunt down along the third base line if I would agree to throw him a fastball "down the pipe" like McClain did for Mantle five years before. I did my part and Kaline laid down a beauty toward third which he beat out for a hit. The problem was, not only did the Tigers NOT take him out of the game, he went on another entire year as a designated hitter, giving me the same hard time at the plate that he had the entire 8 years I had to face him! Thanks Duke! Kaline ended up a lifetime .297 hitter. Should have come out of the game after the bunt Al!

Kaline was a real fan of Mickey's throughout their careers. One time a fan told Kaline that he wasn't half the player Mickey Mantle was. Al's answer to the fan was, "Son, nobody's half as good as Mickey Mantle"!

Sadly enough, but not surprising in lieu of what I've discovered in life, at Kaline's induction into the Baseball Hall of Fame in 1980, in his speech he said, "There's got to be more to life than this". I used to feel that way too and even though I never made the Baseball Hall of Fame, I have good news; there is more to life than the Baseball Hall of Fame! In fact, some of the most miserable people around are members of the Baseball Hall of Fame.

Realizing what Mickey Mantle meant to the Yankees, to baseball, and to all his teammates and friends, I did something that I hated to do, I asked Mickey if I could have something of his to keep as a memento after his last game at Yankee Stadium. He looked around his locker and gave me his last elastic knee wrap. It had "Mick" written on it. It represented to me not only Mickey as a teammate but Mickey the man who endured pain but didn't complain once about it. However, I did ask him one time what his knees felt like. He said, "Like 2 toothaches that never go away".

I had seen Mickey many times since 1968, mostly at Yankee Old Timer games, but I never bothered him for anything. He and Whitey would always have a place to hide after the Old Timers Game, just past the trainer's room to just hang out and catch up on things and not be bothered by current players or their kids. Joe DiMaggio had his own "hiding room" since he and Mickey didn't really get along. Mickey didn't appreciate the fact that Joe made the stadium announcer, Bob Shepherd, introduce him last as the "Yankees greatest living player" or he wouldn't attend Old Times Day. Mickey didn't need that stuff. Now days, the old timers get their own clubhouse and don't mix with the current players in the regular Yankee clubhouse.

Mickey never liked "Mr. October" either. Reggie Jackson liked to try to tie into Mickey's fame as much as he could but Mickey didn't let it happen. Reggie always asked Mickey when he was going to invite him to his golf course in Texas but Mickey never would. Reggie was what Bill Veeck called a "rent a player". Mickey was a lifetime Yankee. Reggie was a "rental".

When I heard that Mickey had died, it didn't surprise me. His illness was highly publicized and some of my Yankee friends who were close to the family had alerted me that Mickey was not well and wouldn't last much longer. What I was concerned about most was about where Mickey would spend eternity.

Having been with Baseball Chapel for 3 years in the early 1980's I had been taught that if a person "accepted Jesus as his (her) personal Lord and Saviour", before he or she dies that they go to Heaven immediately to be with the Lord when they die. Forever! Conversely, if they didn't, they would go to hell; no if, ands, or buts about it. Forever! I didn't know where Mickey stood with the Lord and it bothered me greatly. I knew Mickey wasn't an "angel" on earth (none of us are) and I really was concerned whether or not he had made the right decision, or not.

Mickey had told me at the last Old Timers game I was at with him in New York that if he had known he'd have lived that long that he would have taken better care of himself while he was still playing. No male in the Mantle family had lived beyond 40 years of age prior to Mickey. Mickey said he tried to pack as much into his 40 years as possible! Babe Ruth was said to have squeezed about 150 years into his 50+ years on earth and Mickey wanted to do the same with whatever time he had left.

Mickey, knowing that I had been with the Baseball Chapel ministry joked about being turned down at the gates of Heaven by St. Peter and then being asked whether he would mind autographing a dozen balls for God before he left! It wasn't funny anymore, now it was all real!

On August 13, 1995 I found out from an ex-teammate and friend that Mickey had indeed "accepted Jesus as his Lord and Saviour"! Bobby Richardson let me, and the rest of the world know on ESPN live that day at Mickey's funeral, that Mickey had indeed made the right decision and had gone to be with the Lord in Heaven the second he died--forever! I was elated!

I do not believe that anymore.

CHAPTER **2**

Sorry Thurman!

I was supposed to stay overnight with Thurman Munson on Tuesday night, July 31, 1979 at the hotel the Yankees stayed at in Chicago when they came to play the Chicago White Sox. I had undergone minor surgery in Cleveland, Ohio the week before that "backed up" on me making it impossible to go to Chicago, or anywhere else for that matter.

I would never see Thurman again! He died 2 days later while flying his own jet plane with his 2 flight instructors aboard. The two flight instructors both survived the crash.

The night I was to stay with Thurman, we were going to talk about the Lord and the "born again" thing. He didn't believe in being "born again" and was going to tell me why that night. I was going to tell him about what my teammate and friend on the Texas Rangers, Danny Thompson told me about being "born again" in 1976 which gave me hope despite all the things I had gone through when I was Thurman's teammate in New York and thereafter. We never had that conversation!

I first met Thurman in 1969 at Yankee Stadium when he was brought up from AAA. He was different! Most "rookies" are scared when they first see the Stadium with its history, its size, and what it represents. Not Thurman. It seemed like he had grown up inside the "House that Ruth built"! Actually, Thurman was sort of cocky, almost like he belonged there or something!

At the time, with the hippie 60's ending, baseball was changing a bit too. I first saw it with Stan Bahnsen in 1967.

When I first came up only a year before that in 1966, at the end of the season, Whitey Ford told me, "No Christmas cards kid—you have to be here 5 years before you can send us Christmas cards". He meant it. When Bahnsen first came to the big club, and especially when Thurman arrived, it was if they actually expected the veterans to send them Christmas cards after their first year with the Yankees rather than visa versa.

There was a new group at Yankee Stadium when Thurman arrived in 1969. The pecking order was: Mel Stottlemyre, a quiet leader first, me, Murcer and Roy White were close seconds with Bahnsen close behind. Munson would soon be in the top 5 and climb all the way to the top before long.

Thurman fit right in with everyone from day one. I was sort of the ring leader, like an unofficial traveling secretary for a bunch of guys who were pretty tight. I would always organize "excursions" on long road trips, especially when we had an off day during a road trip. Thurman would beg to be included and I would constantly tease him and tell him we "might consider it" but he had to promise to wait by his hotel door until we decided whether or not he could come along. He would always be invited; he was a gamer on and off the field.

We would limit the group to 5 because it usually involved renting a car and 5 would fit in comfortably. One of our groups of guys would always have to drop out because he was the starting pitcher that day and Thurman would always be the player to be named later as the replacement. It worked out well.

Thurman got 2 nicknames from me. Usually I gave only one

out per player. Thurman deserved 2. The nicest one was "tugs", standing for a tug boat. Thurman was a little bit short but very strong, reminding me of a tug boat. The other one wasn't as flattering, "beer can". That came from the fact that he wasn't circumcised and "it" reminded me of a beer can opener (in the days before the flip top cans). The 2 names were interchangeable.

Thurman didn't care what he looked like in clothes and he could care less what the writers thought about him or anything else for that matter, but when it came to his team and his teammates he was a real favorite and a real gamer, unlike some of the other his Yankee players at that time. Thurman would break up double plays with the best of them or would run over a catcher at home plate if he had to, Murcer and John Ellis did the same and there were a few others. I imagine the Yankees of old were almost all like that. A bunch of our guys weren't.

Thurman was a very proud person yet never bragged. On one of the "excursions" in Texas, I arranged for a car and 5 dirt bikes for us to ride on around Lake Arlington one day before a night game against the Texas Rangers. Once again, we picked Thurman up at his door and off we went, never to return the same again.

We first stopped for a little swim in Lake Arlington because Thurman had to use a restroom which we couldn't find (because there weren't any). Thurman had to go #2 as we all watched as he stood still in the water. He looked a little like a sea pig with his mustache and all and we got a good laugh when a "brown snake" arose from beneath the water next to where Thurman was standing. It didn't swim but it sure did smell! The laughing wasn't over.

The five of us got back on the trail for the rest of the ride. Mel was first, Thurman second, John Ellis third, I was behind John and Stan Bahnsen was behind me. Mel was clipping along at a pretty good pace when he suddenly veered off to the right. Thurman was watching Mel and not the ground and in a moment actually disappeared! He had gone straight over about a 10 foot cliff that

Mel had spotted before any of us! Mel was an avid outdoorsman, unlike the rest of us and had more of a sense for the wild than we did and spotted the cliff. Thurman didn't!

When we all gathered around the pit, we saw Thurman get up as if nothing had happened and say, "Let's go guys"! He had broken both the head light and the tail light in the flight/tumble but was too proud to say he was hurting. When we saw that Thurman was still alive, we laughed so hard our stomach muscles ached for hours! Thurman was not able to catch that night, a rare happening for him!

The person who did have to go behind the plate that night was John Ellis, our back up catcher who ended up taking a spill at 45 miles an hour when his dirt bike couldn't negotiate a sharp curve at such a high rate of speed. John was actually hurt worse than Thurman but didn't want our group to get in trouble for our little "excursion" so John had to "gut it out" that night and hide his cuts, scratches and bruises from the trainer and do the best he could behind the plate to protect our little extra curricular activities. We never told our manager Ralph Houk as we didn't want our little trips to be terminated because we had so much fun!

Because of Thurman's pride, he was perfect for some of my best pranks. I had a theory that the clubhouse, home or road, was "fair game". In other words, whatever came in those doors equally belonged to everyone, especially me. Whether it was a cake, flowers, mail, whatever. On the night that Thurman took his flight into the sand pit at Lake Arlington, I saw him give the visiting clubhouse man an envelope. It wasn't the last day of the road trip so I knew he wasn't paying the clubhouse man his dues. When Thurman went out to the field I asked the clubhouse man if I could have the envelope Thurman just had given him. He gave it to me since I told him I'd take care of mailing it for Thurman. I sure did!

Thurman didn't bring his checkbook to the park that day so he needed someone to write a check for him to the company he was ordering from to enclose in the envelope since mailing cash in the mail was not encouraged. Thurman had ordered a beautiful 12 inch western style holster with an extra long matching leather belt. Thurman had always thought he had a weight problem and knew he would most likely be gaining weight after his playing days were over and wanted to make sure the belt would be big enough for him even into his retirement days ahead.

I felt that I needed to make some revisions to his order. Instead of the western leather design he had ordered, I changed it to a nice smooth black leather finish. I changed the 12 inch size to a 4 inch model, suitable for a Derringer or something similar, and for an added challenge, I made it a left handed holster! The final change was the length of the belt. 28 inches would do in a matching smooth, black leather style. This would insure he couldn't use the belt for anything other than a tourniquet or a watch band or something else little if he decided to keep the belt. I mailed the letter at the hotel later that evening to make sure it would get to its destination.

While Thurman was out on the field trying to loosen up his twisted muscles from the days motorcycle trip, I could just imagine him envisioning how nice his new holster would look on him in a couple of weeks when it arrived at Yankee Stadium. It gave me a nice warm feeling inside.

He wouldn't be the only person waiting for the holster. We all were! I had told a few guys what had just happened and how proud Thurman would be in a few days when his new toy would arrive from Texas. But they had to promise to keep it quiet.

Sure enough, two weeks to the day a package arrived from Texas for Thurman. I, of course, had arrived early that morning like I usually did so I could go over everyone's mail before they arrived. This way, I was able to alert quite a few of the guys so they could secretively observe Thurman opening his package. Everyone knew what was coming so nobody let on that they knew anything about what Thurman had just received.

Thurman quickly opened the package, ready to show its contents to anyone who would look but instead just stared into the box for a second before quickly closing it and putting it behind his seat so nobody could see it. He went ahead and opened other fan mail instead. It was perfect, nobody said anything!

After batting practice Thurman came back into the clubhouse and wrote a note to the holster company on Yankee stationery and put it back into the box. He gave it to Big Pete to send back to Texas because of the screwed up order.

I was watching, of course, from the shadow of my locker across the clubhouse. I went to Big Pete after the game was over and asked him for the box and said that I would take care of it for Thurman. He gave it to me. I wrote a different letter, on Yankee stationery of course, "for" Thurman thanking the company for the precious black holster expressing how happy he was and how proud he will be to use it as a NY Yankee (hoping to get a commercial out of the deal) but there was a problem. He didn't know how to draw left-handed and wondered if they had any brochures on how to learn to draw left-handed? I mailed that letter in a NY Yankee envelope with Thurman's name on it and again waited with "little lefty" (its new name) in my locker nice and safe.

Sure enough, after scanning the Yankee mail one morning I noticed the letter for Thurman from Texas had arrived. I got "little lefty" out of my locker, still in its original mailing box and looking good, and taped the letter to it and placed it on Thurman's locker stool for his arrival. Waiting for the opening were also several well informed players carefully watching #15 once again opening the present he ordered for himself. He opened the box first only to find that "little lefty" had made it back with no changes. This time he suspected something was up but he was no dummy. Thank goodness the players didn't look suspicious and of course he couldn't see me although I saw his every move. He cautiously put the box once again in his locker and set the letter aside to read a bit later, when nobody would be looking.

After the game, when Thurman had left the Stadium, I went and read the letter from the company. It was a beauty! They too were proud to be associated with him and the NY Yankees just as he was proud to be associated with their company but they were very sorry they didn't have any brochures on how to draw left-handed! Thurman had had it! The next day he gave it once again to Big Pete, this time to simply send it back for a refund! Enough was enough!

I once again saw Thurman give "little lefty", box and all to Big Pete for its final trip "home" to Texas for a refund! After a little discussion with Big Pete, I was able to talk him into giving it back to me for safe keeping. It was September already and the season was almost over anyway. "Little lefty" would come home with me to Illinois for the winter.

The next spring came around too quickly. Pitchers and catchers usually go to spring training a week before the other players. Something else went to spring training early—"little lefty"! When Thurman walked into the clubhouse, guess what was on the middle of Thurman's chair in Ft. Lauderdale? He finally had to acknowledge that he had been "had"! Thurman would later tell me a year after I got traded to Cleveland that he dearly missed those days and he'd give up all the money he was getting from the Yankees in 1975 and 1976 to have the good old days back again.

Thurman's pride would get another tweak in Minnesota in 1973 when we played the Twins in a 3 game series in Bloomington, MN. It was a beautiful Saturday morning in Minnesota and all the players were milling around on the sidewalk between where the bus was parked and the hotel. The Twins ballpark was out in Bloomington, MN, which was about a 25 minute trip from the hotel which gave the players little choice but to ride the team bus to and from the ball park due to the large cab fare. Players weren't getting the big bucks like they are today.

Nobody but me was paying attention to a guy who pulled up around the bus and parked momentarily in front of the hotel to deliver a package to someone inside the hotel. Guys were joking around, just talking and having a nice time, when I walked over to a group of our guys and said, "Anybody want a ride out to the park?" Of course they wanted one so I said, "Jump in my car right there and I'll be right out". Four of them climbed into the car and waited, three in the back seat and one in the front! I ran around and told everyone on the sidewalk to "look, those guys are getting into a car they think is mine, don't say anything!" I went and hid around the corner so as to not arouse any suspicion from "my" riders.

A moment later the guy came out of the hotel after having dropped off his package when he realized his car was full of strangers! He just stopped and stared at his car in amazement! When the guys in the car saw him looking at them, they realized that they had been "had" and quietly opened the doors and peeled out slowly, one by one in full view of all their teammates and me. The group included: Thurman Munson, John Ellis, Sparky Lyle, and Steve Kline. In Sparky's book, "The Bronx Zoo", he called me the best prankster he had ever seen. Life was fun!

Thurman was a very bright guy. Making him get into the games even more mentally at times, I would tell him, "Thurman, I need a rest. You call the whole game. I don't want to think today". And he would, and be even better for it. In the past I had learned the hard way that I had to throw the exact pitch I had in mind for each delivery or it could have disastrous results. With Thurman I knew when I asked him to call my game 100% that he could do the thinking for both of us. It worked!

Thurman looked up to Mel Stottlemyre and me because we were good pitchers and we worked well with him behind the plate.

We loved being his teammate because he was a gamer. I never saw a catcher get rid of a ball faster than Thurman behind the plate. He didn't have the best arm I'd ever seen, but he had the quickest release. I even had a thing with him that since I was left-handed, if I saw a guy trying to steal 2nd base during my delivery that I would change any pitch I was going to throw to a fast ball up high and he'd gun them out at 2nd, especially when Gene Michael was playing short. I actually loved it when base runners would try to steal second, it was almost a guaranteed out! Gene, the "stick" could dig anything out of the dirt and get a tag down better than anyone I'd ever seen. He and Thurman made a great combination!

When I had heard that Thurman was killed on my son's birthday, August 2, 1979 I was devastated. Not only was he a dear friend, I was supposed to tell him about how to be get "saved" only two days before he died! I had felt guilty for over 25 years for not having helped "save" Thurman 2 days before he died. I felt that I might have been at least partially responsible for Thurman going to hell. Forever! I felt so guilty that I couldn't even go over and say hello to his wife Diane at a fund raising dinner we both happened to attend in New York City in 2004.

I no longer believe the way I once did about where Thurman is spending eternity. I can, however see why I felt guilty all those years. If "saving" people were my responsibility, how could I, a "saved" person, ever rest knowing I could have helped one more person escape everlasting punishment in hell? There would be no end to the thoughts such as, if had only spent a little more time with them, or if I had given them this, or that little booklet, or whatever? Thank goodness saving souls is not up to us! God's plan is better!

CHAPTER **3**

Bobby Murcer Was a First Round Draft Choice!

Bobby Murcer, like Thurman Munson was a "gamer" and was a friend of mine since we played together in Greensboro, NC in 1965. Bobby was my shortstop at the time, and a good one at that!

Of the "regular position players" on the Yankees during my years there, Bobby and Thurman were what I would call "complete players", what I would consider "real" Yankees. Not only were they excellent players, talent wise, they were team players! Many of the other players on the club were excellent hitters or very good fielders but were lacking in some of the intangible things like taking out a second baseman on a double play or running over a catcher at home plate waiting with the ball to tag them out, like Pete Rose did in the All Star Game I pitched in back in 1970.

Bobby didn't have an uninterrupted career like Mantle or Munson but even though he was traded a couple of times he was a Yankee through and through.

The last time I saw Bobby was in New York at the BAT Dinner (Baseball Assistance Team) in January, 2008. Bobby was the emcee for the dinner like he had promised to do in 2007 but instead had to cancel in order to undergo brain surgery due to a brain tumor the doctors had discovered on Christmas Eve the month before. With what Bobby had gone through in 2007 battling his brain cancer it was a miracle that he was even at the dinner in 2008 much less being the emcee of it!

After the dinner I went over to Bobby and his wife Kay and told him he had done a great job at the dinner and tell him that I had found an old audio tape that we did at a party at my house in 1972 where he and Thurman went around and interviewed everyone. It was over a wireless microphone I had hooked up to an FM Radio that everyone was listening to in our living room, live. The people that were interviewed didn't know that they were being heard in the living room while they were being grilled by both Bobby and Thurman at different times. They put on a great show! I told Bobby I'd make him a copy of the tape which I said was the start of his broadcasting career. It may have been! He said he looked forward to hearing it. (I hope he got to hear it before he died)!

When I saw Bobby up close he looked like he had been beaten up. He had scars from all the brain surgery and had very little hair left. I got flash backs of all the times Bobby got cuts and bruises breaking up double plays and running over catchers at home plate and was reminded of what a battler Bobby really was. I thought, hoped, and prayed that he had made it past the cancer, though I had my fears.

Bobby and I roomed together from time to time but I couldn't take his snoring, especially if I was going to be the starting pitcher the next day. I remember Joe Garagiola doing an interview with me about Mercer's snoring one time that turned out pretty funny. Joe made me make the sounds Bobby made when he snored which was very easy since I'd hear them for about 8 hours at a time each night and couldn't forget them if I wanted to.

The one thing I always felt bad about for Bobby was that he could never be himself. The New York press tagged him the next Mickey Mantle because he was from Oklahoma and tried to tie that in with the clean image and smiling Bobby Richardson whose number they gave him upon Mercer's rejoining the Yankees in 1969. Had Murcer been in any organization other than the Yankees I think he would have ended up with better stats because he wouldn't have been under so much pressure to be someone he wasn't. I'm sure glad he was a Yankee however since we became good friends from 1965 until his death in July, 2008.

Bobby wasn't a devious guy and never pulled anything dirty on anyone but one night he and I felt a little naughty and decided to fill up a big metal wastebasket with water and lean it on someone's hotel door, knock, and run before they saw who did it. After we knocked and began running down the hallway of the hotel we heard a big "swichhhhhh" as the little tsunami poured into the unfortunate hotel guest's room.

As we ran around the corner on our escape route, Bobby ran straight into a Coke machine and hit the floor. I helped him up and we hid in my room for a few minutes until housekeeping finished mopping up the victims room. All Bobby got was a scraped shin, no worse than he got from the ballpark every other day.

I nicknamed Bobby-- "Lemon" in 1966, the only nickname that ever stuck on him. His face was sort of shaped like a lemon and once in a while he would have a sour look to him.

When Bobby got traded to the San Francisco Giants he was crushed! The trade occurred just 3 days after Gabe Paul, the General Manager for the Yankees told him he would be a New York Yankee forever! Gabe was famous for saying, and doing such things. When I told Gabe in 1974 that there were only 2 teams I wouldn't go to, the Cleveland Indians or the Philadelphia Phillies, he said, "Don't worry young man, we wouldn't do that to you"! Before that week was over, 3 teammates and I were headed to Cleveland in part of a blockbuster trade. When Gabe told Mel Stottlemyre in spring training, 1975 that he should take his time getting his ailing shoulder in shape, Mel found himself being called into Gabe's office to sign his "pink sheet" (his release) on March 29th, 7 days before the end of spring training, just in time so the Yankees wouldn't have to pay him his whole years salary.

Bill Veeck told me that Gabe Paul was known as the "smiling cobra"! Do you wonder why?

The spring after Murcer was traded to the Giants, I never saw an unhappier player in my life! I was with the Cleveland Indians then when I first saw Bobby in his new uniform. When we played the Giants in a spring training game I couldn't believe how "out of place" Bobby looked in his Giants uniform. His nickname, "lemon" really fit him well through the experience although the Giant players weren't aware of the nickname.

Bobby was then traded to the Chicago Cubs before the 1978 season where he didn't look quite as out of place as he did in a Giant uniform. He still didn't look right in a Cub uniform either; he was born to be a Yankee! He finally got back where he belonged with the Yankees in 1979 but with some hurt feelings in the process. I'm actually surprised that Bobby went into the broadcast booth in 1983 after what Gabe had done to him and I'm also surprised Mel went back to coach for the Yankees after his "surprise release" by Gabe in 1975. I guess the Yankee pinstripes are more compelling than some of the people that head up their front offices!

Bobby and I used to bite the skin on the inside of our mouths and show it to each other seeing who could bite off the biggest piece of skin, like little kids would do. After I was traded from the Yankees I used to bite a piece of skin off the inside of my cheek and put it on a piece of paper and scotch tape it down (so it wouldn't shrink) and send it to him. Bobby enjoyed my "gifts" and my sick sense of humor but in time, his wife Kay recognized my writing and would toss out some of my "flesh offerings" before Bobby could get them.

Sparky Lyle liked my "gifts" too. Once in a while I would consume a very large pizza and sometimes (Kids: don't read the rest of this sentence) purge afterward so I didn't have to wear it the next day.

I would take a picture of the aftermath and send it on to my left-handed buddy, Sparky Lyle to enjoy. He would get a big kick out of my mailings, I know, he's told me so. Sparky was a player's player, the guy you wanted as your brother and especially as your teammate!

Our whole core group of players enjoyed those days even though we didn't win any pennants. By the time the winning finally came back to Yankee Stadium in 1976, only Sparky, Thurman, and Roy White were still there from our original core group but the fun was gone. At least Bobby got to come back for some of the winning in 1980 and 81 but it wasn't the same as the good old days from 1969 to 1974! I'm happy for Bobby and his wife Kay that he got back in pinstripes and for Mel and his wife Jean for that matter. My new wife and I would have loved it too!

I really tried coming back as a color man for the Yankees but when Gene Michael, the general manager of the Yankees then, asked George Steinbrenner about it he said, "Oh, we couldn't do that", inferring that I was bad for the clean image the Yankees portrayed! I do know the Yankees were very upset that when my wife swapping situation hit the papers in March of 1973 and the publicity it garnered blew away the intended headlines planned for the day that Bobby Murcer had signed for $100,000 a year, the 1st player to do so since Mickey Mantle retired back in 1968! Because of me, Bobby's signing didn't even make the first page!

The first game after Thurman's death Bobby almost single-handedly won the game for the Yankees knocking in all 5 runs in a 5-4 victory at Yankee Stadium. It drained Bobby physically and emotionally and brought tears to his eyes along with thousands of other fans at the ballpark and over the airwaves. It was a very fitting for Bobby to honor his buddy Thurman in such a way.

After my marriage situation became public in 1973, my new wife and I went out constantly with the Munson's, Murcer's, and Stottlemyre's.

My ex-wife, Marilyn never really hung around with the other wives much other than with Jim Bouton's wife Bobby, but my new wife was very athletic and outgoing and really enjoyed being around all the other players wives. I often wonder what life would have been like had my "new wife" and I had started out together from the beginning?

When Bobby Murcer didn't return to the booth at the beginning of the season in 2008 I became suspicious that his old problem had come back to haunt him. It had! His brain cancer had almost run the same course that it had in another baseball friend of mine, Dick Howser back in the 1980's. Howser too ended up dying of brain cancer in 1987 after a year battling the disease. Unfortunately, as it turned out, my nickname for Howser was "Skull", because of his intelligence. I believe if Howser didn't get cancer and die that he would have been the best manager of the 20th century! He was a tremendous person and manager!

Bobby hid his prognosis from just about everyone since Dr. Saadah first shocked him with his words, "Bobby, you have a brain tumor" on Christmas Eve, 2006. Bobby's family showed their reliance on God the night before his operation to remove the tumor when Kay's brother Dwaine led the family in a devotional based on Deuteronomy 31:6, "be strong and courageous, do not be afraid or terrified because of them, for the Lord your God goes with you. He will 'never leave you or forsake you'!" That verse became Bobby's personal mantra up to the last day he spent on earth!

Bobby never told the public that Dr. Weinberg had given him about 14 months to live after his operation on December, 2006 but admitted that God had given Kay and him the strength to guide them to the end! At an autograph show at Yogi Berra's Museum in New Jersey in the spring of 2008 Bobby, was visibly worn out. He even nodded off a couple of times during the show. Poor thing! Rest would finally come to Bobby on July 12, 2008 but not before he told listeners on the radio during his last appearance over the air waves on May 2nd that "God has just blessed me, what can I say?"

As far as Bobby's salvation was concerned, I never gave it a second thought like I did with Mantle and especially with Munson. I had been told by several people that Bobby was a "true believer" and together with what I now know, he is covered either way! As far as Heaven is concerned, Bobby was a "first round draft choice" when he died. That's as good as it gets, and he knew it! His uniform will either be like the old fashioned ones in Babe Ruth's day, with no numbers on them, or, we'll all have #1's on our backs. Ironically, Bobby's old number with the Yankees was #1 most of his career! Win/win.

CHAPTER 4

Bouton Died!

Jim Bouton and Mike Kekich were probably my "deepest" friends during the time we were teammates on the Yankees together, but not afterwards. They both seemed to have another dimension to them that I didn't have but wished I had. They did, and said what they wanted and didn't care what people thought about it. I could only imagine the legacies they'd have left behind had they put up career stats similar to Sandy Koufax and Don Drysdale!

Bouton was a college graduate from the Midwest which set him apart from most of the Yankee players other the Steve Hamilton, Tom Tresh and me. Jim was different. Not a "Forrest Gump" different, but always a little ahead of his time mixed in with being a nonconformist. Jim actually related better with the writers, who were all college graduates themselves than with any of his Yankee teammates—other than me.

I learned right away that spring in 1966 that Jim had always wanted to date the sister (Elaine) of my best friend in college, Steve Smoot, and was basically a Midwesterner at heart like I was. We hit it off right away my rookie year. Other than my initial tryout with the Yankees in Chicago in 1963, I had never as much as spoken to any "big leaguer" much less be a teammate of theirs. Jim helped me to feel comfortable during that first spring and sort of took me under his wing.

After Jim saw me pitch in a couple of outings in actual spring training games in Ft. Lauderdale he told me that he thought I actually had an outside chance of making club that year. It was scary to hear but it was the very reason I was invited to spring training in the first place. It was just nice hearing it from someone who was there and had been there for a few years. Little did I know, the chance I did have was that Jim's record the year before was only 4-15 because of his ailing right shoulder and it would be his spot that I'd be taking in the starting rotation that year! It was a little like a Wally Pipp story or sorts. (Wally Pipp sat out a game for the Yankees in 1925 and never started another game there for the Yankees—Lou Gehrig filled his spot).

Jim saw more in life and in living than the other guys did. He saw things even while riding on the team bus from the hotels to the ball parks. Things like little kids playing with their dogs and stuff like that others missed out on because they were to busy talking about their home run the day before or how last nights hangover felt. Jim taught me about life as well as teaching me how to throw a "palm ball" which really helped me on the mound the rest of my career.

My dad always liked me hanging around with guys like Bouton because they had fun in life and enjoyed a good laugh. Jim wasn't much for little petty pranks like Mickey and some of the other guys were into like giving someone a hot foot and other than putting powder in Joe Pepitone's hair dryer in 1967 Jim liked the big stuff. My dad wouldn't have appreciated a couple of things Jim and I almost did while we were teammates however. One of those proposed things was to jump on a freight train in Cleveland one night after Jim had a rough outing on the mound and riding to Chicago like hobos did and then asking my dad to drive us back to Cleveland the next day in time for the game. I chickened out on that one because I didn't want to get in trouble and would never want to be late for anything, ever, much less a ballgame! I must have inherited a "late gene" from my dad as well as his sense of humor. Bobby Murcer had the "late gene" too, he couldn't stand to be late for anything either.

Another one my dad wouldn't have liked was the one we planned for the Shriners Convention that wouldn't have been on their itinerary the weekend we shared a hotel in Detroit with them in 1967. Jim always found the Shriners annoying with all their antics on their once a year getaways even though it was just like what we did 26 times or more a year on our very own road trips! Jim thought their red "circus hats" looked ridiculous along with their motorcycles and he wanted to give them something to remember from their Detroit trip that year!

Jim had it planned that we would pick a floor 2 floors down from where our rooms were and find a fire hose close to a stairwell and wait until everyone got drunk and then hosing them down-- big time. We were going to douse as many as we could and then run up the stairway to our floor and hide in our rooms until the fire department finished shutting off the alarms making it safe for us to leave our rooms without being caught. Jim felt that if we'd go down stairs, we might get caught but going up stairs was a different story. Jim always thought ahead. I chickened out on that one too!

I wish I had Jim's nerve but I didn't. He told me that one time in spring training when he was holding out after having had a great year the year before that he sat right behind home plate in the stands during a spring training game by himself while the owners circled him trying to intimidate him into signing for what they offered him in full view of his teammates. They thought that Jim would be embarrassed and that it would break him down. Forget it, his nickname was "bulldog" at the time and he didn't get it for nothing.

In those days, players were at a huge disadvantage in that they had only two choices when it came to contract time: sign, or quit!

If you quit, you couldn't play for any other organization, ever! Bill Veeck told me in 1977 that the owners should have negotiated a different agreement before they were forced to do it by the players association in the mid 70's. It is ridiculous what advantage the players have today in the free agency market but as Bill Veeck said, it all stemmed from the owners unwillingness to amend the old reserve clause until they were forced into doing it later at a much greater price.

Once I got to the Yankees, Bouton's old nickname "bulldog" had to change. Jim has a rather pointy nose and along with the long crew cut he wore then, he looked to me a little like a rooster so—"Rooster" it was!

I looked at Jim like the big brother I never had. Speaking of "big brother", Jim was a nonconformist and didn't like traditional rules of any kind, especially those that had evolved throughout baseball from nowhere. That worried the Yankee coaching staff, in particular, Frank Crosetti and Jim Turner immensely, especially since they were both convinced that Bouton was an actual communist. Crosetti actually told Jim to his face one day during a disagreement they were having in the clubhouse that Jim was really a communist!

I ended up having the best win/loss record for the 1966 season, and even though it was only 12-11 we had come in last place that year, the first time that had happened to the Yankees since 1912.

1967 was different however. Although I had planned on winning 20 games in 1967, I didn't win a game the first half of the season, losing 8 in a row before my first win which wasn't until July! Jim and I roomed together at the time so the Yankee brass naturally thought he was having a bad influence on me. They decided to separate us. They did in a back door manner by saying that since Jim had been a Yankee for a few years that he deserved a room of his own on road trips like Mickey and Whitey always had, a promotion of sorts. The Yankees didn't take the fact into account that I didn't get a run while I was on the mound for 35 2/3 innings in a row which automatically accounted for 5 of those 8 losses but preferred to blame Jim instead. Oh well, Jim appreciated the single room although it was apparent that the Yankees long term plans for Jim were narrowing, communism notwithstanding.

In 1968, my wife and I rented a house from Jim in New Jersey. He had been investing in income property for a couple of years by then, another one of Jim's smart moves. He even taught my ex-wife, Marilyn and me how to invest in property which eventually made her a millionaire after she ended up with 2 of our better properties from our divorce in 1974. She was very smart to hold on to those properties over the years whereas I had to sell mine in order to pay for the legal fees incurred in the divorces; mine, Marilyn's and my new wife's. At least my sons are benefiting from Marilyn's excellent business mind.

Jim and I rode together to Yankee Stadium a lot of times. What an experience! If you have taken drivers training in high school you might remember being taught to drive "defensively". Jim is the reason; he is the "offense"! Jim would use the safety lane between the left lane of the highway and the cement barriers as his "private" passing lane! When he used it, dust, coke cans, and cigarette butts would go flying everywhere but it worked—for Jim. If you've been on Route 4 in Jersey close to New York City you know what I'm talking about!

Speaking about cars, every time the Yankees would go to Oakland Jim and I would rent a car and go to Sausalito or Berkley for the day to see the "hippies". Jim liked them but I was scared of them. They had all that hair and were so dirty looking. On the way, we would have the radio playing Mexican music just to make our trips a little different. I still do it to this day although it's hard to find Mexican music in the places I live now, especially in upstate New York. It's impossible to find in Wyoming.

Jim loved to argue! On one road trip alone, he took on a "Satan worshipper" all dressed in black sitting under a black umbrella in

Haight Ashbury on the first leg of our road trip and on the last leg of the trip locked horns with a "street preacher" to even things out. Jim "won" both debates but almost got us chased in the process by the people listening to the street preacher in Kansas City. I had to intervene and get us out of there before were attacked! Maybe that's why people say not to talk about religion or politics!

In 1968, Jim got a rare start in Baltimore but got killed! Rather than go out and drown his sorrows, which Jim never did, he decided to celebrate. He asked me to go out to dinner with him to a very nice restaurant in Baltimore. Jim taught me a new order that night, "Chateau Brianne for two--for one" all for him of course. I had lobster.

Then, on June 15, 1968 I had the worst day of my baseball life, Bouton "died"! It was a term I had coined a few years before to signify when a player got traded or released (fired). Jim called me from his room in Oakland with the words I never wanted to hear. He said, "I died"! I was hoping that he was kidding but he wasn't, the Yankees had sold him to the Seattle organization that would field a team that would become the Seattle Pilots the next season. Jim's departure created a big "void" for me for the rest of the year. A lefthander from the Dodgers would fill that void for me in 1969.

In 1969, the Yankees were in Seattle to play the Pilots when a big fight broke out on the field at Sicks Stadium. In baseball, tradition says that if a fight breaks out, everyone goes out to the field to help their teammates, from both teams. Jim came running in from the Seattle bull pen and I ran out from the Yankee dugout to see how we could avoid getting punched when we spotted each other and acted as if we were wrestling while the "big dogs" on the Yankees (John Ellis, Bill Burback and Frank Fernandez) were facing off with Seattle's thugs (Fred Talbot, Gene Brabender and Jack Aker) on another part of the infield. Jim and I fell to the ground laughing and rolled around a little until we were surrounded by 4 men in blue, the umpires! They felt it was safer to be around us than around the gladiators hacking away at each other close to the mound!

Jim was writing his famous book, Ball Four, during the 1968 season and although it didn't come out until 1970, I felt offended when it did. He only said good things about me in the book, I hear, but I thought we were closer friends than that and that he should have trusted me with the knowledge of his impending book. I think it was his co-writer, Leonard Schecter that told him he shouldn't tell me or anyone about the book, especially since Leonard was sharing the profits with Bouton and he didn't want anything to disrupt the release of the book. In my opinion that did damage to our friendship. Things were never quite the same between us after that.

I still haven't read the book! I was friends with all the players he named in the book and Jim as well so I felt the only way to maintain both sets of friends was not to read the book. I may do it someday but it will probably be when I'm tucked way back in a nursing home somewhere. I hear it's hilarious though!

After his book came out, Bouton was barred from the Yankee clubhouse and informally from a lot of clubhouses even though Mickey and Whitey were out of baseball by then. Their allegiances from other players weren't gone however as many players felt uncomfortable around Jim since he had turned in his fellow teammates for a profit.

Jim joined a TV station in New York after he retired the first time after the 1970 season. He knew I'd do an interview with him even though the other Yankees wouldn't, so he and his film crew flew down to Ft. Lauderdale and we shot the piece with Jim standing outside the ballpark and me standing inside, with the fence between us. It was a pretty neat interview.

I did one other thing for Jim the day after our "wife swapping" situation broke in the media on March 5, 1973. It was a TV shoot in the backyard of my rented home in Ft. Lauderdale talking about what had happened in our families. That was the last interview I ever did about the "situation" and it was a favor to Jim because of our friendship.

I saw Jim in the early 2000's and asked him his opinion on whether or not I should do a book. He said he wouldn't. Now we're even!

Jim is a pretty stubborn guy and nobody tells him what to do. He's a bit like Thurman Munson was in that he is the "captain of his own ship" and will do things his own way no matter what. Coupling that with what I now know about salvation, I'm afraid that Jim will have to take a little "dip" in the "lake of fire" for a while. How long, only God knows but I'm certain Jim is not a first round draft choice yet like Mantle and Murcer were, at least at this point! On Jim's behalf however, he once told me that if were dropped off in the middle of the ocean, but knew the direction the shore was, he would never stop swimming until he got there. He also told me that if he didn't know what direction a shore was, he'd quit swimming right away and be done with it (life). All Jim needed was a direction!

My advice: keep swimming, the shore is straight ahead and you still have time to move up to a "first round draft choice"!

CHAPTER 5

Kekich, The Left-handed Bouton

I was teaching in the Physical Education Department at Northern Illinois University during the off season of 1968 when I read that the Yankees had picked up a hard throwing left-handed pitcher, Mike Kekich, from the Dodgers for a right-handed power hitter of sorts, Andy Kosco. The Yankees were trying to add another pitcher to the roster since Al Downing hadn't been used much and Jim Bouton had been sold to Seattle during the 1968 season.

When I heard about the trade I didn't react one way or the other since I had never seen Mike pitch and Andy was no big asset to the Yankees during the 1968 season, nor was Andy some young phenom that might blossom into a Reggie Jackson or something. When Mike arrived in spring training in February, 1969 I knew I had my old friend, Jim Bouton back. This time in a younger, left handed body!

This time, instead of the older brother I'd always wanted, as was Bouton, I got the younger brother I always wanted. Mike. This time around, instead of being the student, I'd be the teacher. At least baseball wise. Mike had many of the same mannerisms that Bouton had, along with the "wild side", from spending many years in California.

Like Bouton, Mike and I hit is off right away. Even though we both threw left-handed, we both ate right-handed, maybe the only thing we really had in common other than we were now teammates. We might have been compared with the characters in the movie the "Odd Couple" with Jack Lemon and Walter Matthau.

Mike was a power pitcher who had received a rather large signing bonus from the Dodgers and threw like Sandy Koufax and I was a finesse pitcher who signed for a meager bonus ($9,000) in 1963 and pitched a lot like Yankee great Whitey Ford. Mike tried to strike everyone out while I simply tried to get guys out as quickly as possible. I always thought: why not throw just 1 or 2 pitches to get someone out instead of using 5 or 6 pitches per hitter trying to rack up strike outs. Ironically, later on in our careers I blew out my shoulder (in 1976) and he hasn't wrecked his even to this day as far as I know! (Maybe the fact that I pitched 1,300 more innings in the big leagues than Mike had a little something to do with it?)

In 1969, Mike came to Ft. Lauderdale for his first spring training as a Yankee, driving a neat little sports car, a convertible of course, and wore a leather sports cap to fit the part and make a statement--he was from California. And a lefthander to boot! On the other hand, I drove a Plymouth station wagon and the only hat I wore was a Yankee cap--on the field.

Mike never brought his wife or children to spring training with him. I always did. He felt that the six weeks in spring training were "his", both to get in shape for the season and to have some fun along the way. I never gave it a thought but probably didn't have a choice anyway. When Mike first joined the Yankees, he had a daughter 2 years old and I had a son the same age.

Like Bouton had done for me, I took it upon myself to do for Mike. I took him under my wing. Since he wasn't a Yankee "product" from the start, like most of us were (from the Yankee farm system), the guys naturally were a little standoffish toward Mike when he first arrived in Ft. Lauderdale in 1969. Since I was almost a "veteran" by then and was part of the small group that the Yankees counted on to bring them back to prominence, I carried some weight on the team. I used that weight and my friendships on the team to try to bring Mike into the fold. And unlike Bouton, the players trusted me which made it easier for Mike to be "one of us".

There was only one slight problem bringing Mike into our "group", however. Just like Bouton, Mike enjoyed arguing and doing things his own way. It didn't seem to be that much of a problem with the players but the coaches and the manager were a different story, especially after having to put up with Bouton the last few years. They didn't want to have to deal with another "comrade". And this time a left-handed one! Because of that, the coaches were always looking at Mike through a magnifying glass.

Having been around for a while and having had some good seasons behind me by that time and not being an arguer, I knew how to work the system and not cause waves while still quietly doing things my own way. Kekich and Bouton couldn't. And although it cost them from time to time, I admired that quality in them both; they did what sometimes I would have liked to have done.

With Mantle and Bouton both gone in 1969, the Yankees hoped to be bringing on a new era for the franchise, one that they had been accustomed to before—winning. Thurman Munson would be making his debut as the Yankee catcher of the future and Bobby Murcer was coming back, after his stint in the service, and it looked like Kekich could fit in to help what was a pretty good starting rotation: Stottlemyre, me, Bahnsen, Downing, and Kekich.

Mike had a very good fastball, velocity wise, and a decent curve ball but lacked another off speed pitch just like me my first year. Bouton had taught me how to throw a palm ball, (a pitch that you hold in with your palm with your thumb and little finger and just 'pitch it' out of your throwing hand giving it a top spin which acts like a changeup/splitter combination). I picked it up immediately and used it in the first game I pitched after mastering it. I showed it to Mike, who also learned it right away, which helped him become a decent starting pitcher even though his overall control wasn't that good. I'm sure our pitching coach, Jim Turner, wouldn't have liked it if he knew it was Bouton's palm ball but since I had taught Mike "my" pitch, it was OK.

Speaking about control, Mike had started a game in Detroit one night that my dad happened to be attending. Mike lost his grip on the ball during his delivery and the ball ended up sailing into the stands and hitting a lady in the breast. The lady was fine, so it was fortunately only funny, but was reminiscent of the times Ryan Duran would come in to relieve a pitcher and throw a warm up pitch all the way to the screen behind home plate to intimidate the hitter waiting in the on deck circle to face him (he threw 100 MPH and had glasses as thick as Coke bottles)! Ryan did it on purpose. Mike didn't.

My dad liked having me pal around with Mike, the "new Bouton", and knew how much I had missed Jim since he was traded away in the middle of the 1968 season. My dad appreciated having fun in life and Mike even had more fun than Jim. Jim was always working on some project, or book as it turned out, whereas Mike just had "happy-go-lucky fun", maybe even too much at times.

Mike and I would go to piano bars on the road from time to time whenever we could find them. He liked to sing and I liked to harmonize. Mike could even yodel with the best of them. Our favorite pub was in Detroit. Unfortunately, the club burned down in 1971. One of our favorite coaches, Jim Hegan, also went there and even though he didn't drink he just took pleasure in hearing us sing it up. Coach Hegan wasn't hunting for "comrades". He just enjoyed being a good guy, passing some time on the road.

Just like Bouton had expanded my horizons outside the ballpark, so did Mike. One day, Mike talked me into going gliding with him on an off day in California. We went to Lake Elsinore, noted for its gusty winds which were tailor made for gliding. It was an experience that I never would have done on my own but nothing like what he would take me on next. This time under the ocean in the Keys in Florida during the next spring training. I saw what a daredevil Mike was when he actually chased a Manta Ray as big as a car down about 25 feet! Diving was really peaceful, much more so than gliding and much less dangerous even though Steve Irwin wouldn't agree if he were still alive today.

Then it was sailing in Ft. Lauderdale on a catamaran we rented. I can't believe we weren't injured or killed on that one when we were caught by high winds and high waves that tossed us into the shallow water at 100 miles an hour (or so it seemed). We didn't get a scratch. It wasn't our time yet!

The first time I met Mike's wife was after a game at Yankee Stadium in 1969. It was drizzling that night and Mike and I walked up together from the clubhouse and went out the stadium office door where his wife had been parked waiting for him. He introduced me to her. She was seated on the passenger side of the car. We said our "nice to meet you" stuff when his wife said, "It's raining, don't get wet" and I said, for some reason, "don't worry, it's worth it". Little did I know at the time how much it would be worth!

Mike would always feel bad for abused and neglected wives wherever he saw them. Whenever he would see a situation where he thought that might be the case he would mention it to me—"abused and neglected", he'd say while he was shaking his head. He always wanted to help them out.

Mike became part of what I called the "Nursery". It was comprised of only starting pitchers although we'd let Thurman Munson in once in a while. It included me, Stottlemyre, Kekich, Bahnsen, and Steve Kline in 1970 and Doc Medich in 1971 when Bahnsen got traded to the White Sox. The main characters were me, Kekich, and Bahnsen. I even had tee shirts printed up saying the "Nursery" on them. It was good, clean fun--constantly.

When Sparky Lyle came to the Yankees in 1973 he was

automatically inducted since he was a perfect "nursery mate" for all of us!

I was seldom the victim of a "sting", but did most of the stinging! I was the one who caused guys to get caught "in the act" when I was the one who actually started the ball rolling without their knowledge.

I would sneak into the clubhouse during a game when nobody was paying attention, do something to one of the guy's personal belongings in his locker, then I'd tell that guy that I had just seen the other guy doing something to his stuff. I'd suggest that he might want to check out his locker to see the damage the "other" guy had done. While he went into the clubhouse to see the damage, I would tell the other guy that so and so was doing something to his locker and he'd better check it out. He would then rush into the clubhouse to see the other guy "doing" his locker and catch him red handed. It was a blast! They never really caught on until Sparky's book "The Bronx Zoo" came out. By then it was too late! There were always 2 innocent guys doing each others stuff while I sat on the bench enjoying the ball game on the field knowing there was a skirmish going on inside the clubhouse that I started.

Guys regularly received precious plants from friends and relatives for special occasions delivered to the clubhouse. The delicate plants were automatically doused with rubbing alcohol while the players were out on the field. Vaseline got gobbed by the pound on the back of guys heads. Large hardened, uncuttable locks were snapped onto the loops or buttonholes of expensive clothing with no key available to unlock it—anything and everything went. No holds barred! It was nonstop! That's why Munson said in 1976 that he'd have given anything to be back to the "good old days"! The "nursery" was instrumental in most of the off the field laughing.

The time Mike got the maddest was on a road trip that began in California and ended in Milwaukee. While we were in California, Mike bought one of the first waterbeds anyone had ever seen.

California got everything first, good or bad. His mistake was showing it to a couple of the guys in the clubhouse in Anaheim when he was packing it up for the trip back east.

Once the word got out, something had to be done, especially since Mike was so proud of his new, mod purchase. That "something" was that since he was so proud of it, everyone else should at least get a chance to see what he was so proud of! Everyone did. Bahnsen paid one of the clubhouse kids $10 to take it up to the top of the scoreboard in centerfield and hang it next to the American flag, about 50 feet up from the ground.

I was pitching that day and was warming up in the bullpen right under the scoreboard when I heard Mike's spikes scraping on the metal stairs as he headed up to retrieve his precious waterbed that was now on "display" next to the American flag for all to admire. Even though I wasn't directly involved in the caper, since I was pitching that day, it was sure enjoyable seeing Mike panic trying to save his new purchase.

I went to the dugout after I finished my warm-ups and got to see, along with 40,000+ fans and the TV audience from New York and the coaching staff, Mike untangling his waterbed from the top of the scoreboard while the National Anthem was playing as the American flag and Mike's waterbed waved gently in the wind together! It may have cost me the game, however, since my concentration wasn't quite "there", hearing Mike climb up the scoreboard stairs and seeing how upset our manager and pitching coach got during the National Anthem before the game even started. I only lasted 3 innings that day, something that rarely occurred.

Because of it, Mike tried to have Bahnsen's and my luggage sent to Japan from the airport in Milwaukee after the final game of the series to get even with us for the waterbed hanging. The bags were intercepted in Dallas after we had discovered they were missing and ended up back in New York the next day. Even though our bags never got to Japan, Mike did a few years later when he pitched for the Nippon Hams in Japan while he was trying to prolong his career in baseball. I would have liked pitching over there too but my arm died in the summer of 1976 before I could try something like that.

Mike was always interested in medical things and when Doc Medich came up to the Yankees in 1971 Mike had someone to answer all of his medical questions. Once in a while, Mike and I would pose as doctors at upscale pubs on road trips if we could find a couple of young ladies that had questions we could help them with. Mike knew enough of the terminology to get by with unless the problem involved gynecological issues. He was the "real doctor" while I usually played the role of a psychologist since many of those issues are in the "gray" anyway. I could generally dance around the real issues like "Slick Willie" (Clinton) and not be specific about anything. Mike would play the role and drink brandy out of an official brandy "sniffer" and I'd just have a plain old Lite Beer because I didn't care about the facade and anyway, only drove a station wagon and really didn't inhale! Funny how life works sometimes. Who would have known that one day Mike would become a real doctor, even though his designation was only good in Mexico. But at least he was introduced at an Old Timers Game as "Doctor" Mike Kekich. 'Doc' (George) Medich was sure proud of Mike since he did a lot of tutoring for him during their Yankee days together.

One time, on a trip to Detroit, Mike and I brought a couple of our "patients" back to our room. We joked that it was a double date even though, of course, we were both married men. Oddly enough it didn't bother either one of our consciences since it was "just for fun". Our wives, though, may not have seen the humor in it if we had told them!

For my part, I was beginning to realize that I was growing apart from Marilyn. There were more and more things I couldn't talk about with her and at the same time began realizing there was something missing in my life. Although we didn't discuss it directly, I remember Marilyn getting me a book called "The Marriage Art". It focused mainly on "making love" (sex), a sort of "how to" book. I realize now that she was trying to tell me that I didn't "have it". I had never really thought about it before but I'm sure she was right but I really didn't want to do anything about it. I was content the way I was.

I should have figured out during Mike's and my "double date" in Detroit that Mike may have read the book Marilyn wanted me to read. Or even wrote it because I observed that he was good at the "art". It should have dawned on me that maybe that was the reason Mike always commented about women who were abused and neglected. I don't think I ever abused Marilyn but I'm sure I "neglected her", at least in "that" way.

Mike and I were seeing a lot of each other and during the spring of 1971, he actually helped potty train my youngest son with "Junior Mints". He was at our house almost daily during that spring, sometimes parking his sports car on our porch so we couldn't open our front door.

My kids and Marilyn sure liked having him around. He was fun!

I met Mike's mom in Oakland one time on a road trip. She was really fun too. She and Mike took turns filming each other on one of the trolley cars in San Francisco. One scene would be of his mom running after the trolley car and the next scene would have her in front of the trolley trying to get away from it. It was hilarious. I saw where he got his sense of humor.

On that same trip Mike rented a car and thought he'd save some money by jacking the car up and running it in reverse for over an hour to take miles off of the odometer. When he turned the car in to the dealership he found out that he had unlimited mileage and had burned up a tank of gas for nothing! Lefthander!

I kept trying to help Mike fit in with our core group on the Yankees and to help him as much as I could on the mound. Our pitching coach was total "old school" and Mike was "total" California. Not a good mix. But I was right in the middle of having 5 very good years in a row and the coach knew what good friends Mike and I were.

This prompted him to let a few of the things slide that could have caused problems for Mike had he not been my close friend.

I was a little jealous of Mike's personal life because of his wife's easy going nature. She was also very athletic, having been a very popular cheerleader back in high school in California. Marilyn's closest brush with sports was her stint on the rifle team at her high school in Rockford, Illinois, involving the ROTC program there. Mike's wife even ran cross country competitively in New Jersey during the season to keep in shape. Marilyn wasn't interested in sports of any kind.

Mike was allowed by his wife to stay at the ballpark for a while after home games to mingle with the fans after games. I, on the other hand, more or less, felt like I had to and get home as fast as humanly possible to be with Marilyn. Even though I was a little envious of Mike, I never gave it a second thought that I might end up not being with Marilyn and my sons someday. I just wanted to do the best I could in baseball to make our life as financially secure as I could. I planned on retiring when the time was right and being the baseball coach at my alma mater, NIU, and live happily ever after with Marilyn and my 2 sons.

I suggested to Marilyn that we buy a lot by a lake in Wisconsin and put a cabin on it as a "get away". Her folks had done that along with her aunt and uncle a few years before. Marilyn nixed it. It was just one of many "nixings" I'd get from her which, for me, took much of the fun and spontaneity out of my life. (I don't blame her for all of it since I allowed it to continue, but it was a cloud I felt hanging over our heads, gathering moisture, unbeknownst to her, or me for that matter).

Once I was out of baseball, I couldn't afford to teach or coach due to my heavy financial responsibilities supporting two families. The fact that the baseball team at NIU was no longer an official team sport meant that there was no coaching opportunity there for me either. I tried to get into announcing but I was semi black-balled due to the highly publicized divorce I went through. Clinton hadn't gotten into office yet to set the pace for the country's morals so I had a shadow over me keeping me in the closet. Had the "slickster" been in office during my "hay day" I might have ended up as the Baseball Commissioner! Who knows? My guy, Nixon, had to resign because of Watergate so there was little hope for me to be employed over the airwaves in those days.

Speaking of Bill Clinton, I think he would have been a great teammate, especially on the road. He is left-handed and has a great sense of humor. He would have fit in well with Sparky Lyle, Mike, and me! Hillary seems very scary, however! You never know if she's a Yankee fan, a Cubs fan or what. She sure is good at playing the stock market however! The "slickster" would have helped to take some of the heat off of Mike and me as we waded through our public relations fiasco, alone, in 1973! I wonder if Monica made any road trips?

During my last year in baseball I did become a "born again" believer. It helped me mentally and spiritually. I did share that with Mike while he was with the Seattle Mariners in 1977, but he said "thanks, but no thanks" to the Jesus thing. I also saw him one time in Puerto Rico where I met his new wife, Michelle, a very pretty girl from Corpus Christi, Texas.

As far as Mike's belief in God is concerned, I heard from one of my sons that Mike was not a "believer" (in Jesus) and certainly didn't attend a Church. Not that my sons assessment has anything to do with Mike's salvation or about his future plight in the hereafter, but I would be surprised, knowing Mike, that he, or Bouton would attend any Church or Synagogue unless they had been the founders of it.

Like Bouton, I'm afraid Mike will be taking a "dip", maybe even a "swim" in the "lake of fire" for a long time. He is pretty bullheaded. The two of them, (Bouton & Kekich) might even surface as a quienella (a gambling term for 2 players, or dogs, horses, etc. finishing first and second, or second and first in a race or contest).

I don't know how they'd finish, either #56-- 1st and #18-- 2nd, or #18-- 1st and #56-- 2nd . Kekich's number with the Yankees was #18; Bouton's was #56.

The good news, guys, is that there's still time to get in on a perfecta ticket (another gambling term for 1st and 2nd place in the exact specified order), or better yet, in a virtual tie as first round draft choices like Mantle and Murcer! Stranger things have happened; like me having become a "first round draft choice" for instance! It's never too late!

CHAPTER 6

O.J. Simpson & Me—Guilty!

Almost all of us remember O.J. Simpson's acquittal back in the mid 90's for allegedly killing his ex-wife Nicole Brown Simpson and Ron Goldman. Just about everyone felt justice had not been served. On the weekend of October 4th, 2008, most felt a little vindication when O.J. was found guilty of all 12 charges against him in a Las Vegas casino robbery in which he tried to get back some of the memorabilia he felt "belonged to him".

The fact is, most people want "justice", especially if it concerns someone other than themselves. The O.J. case is a great example.

I can remember sitting in our bedroom in East Dundee, Illinois, with my wife and 2 of our daughters when O.J.'s "not guilty" verdict was read. We couldn't believe it! All that DNA evidence and everything else and he's innocent? We didn't think so, nor did many other people. The country felt cheated!

When my "situation" hit the papers on March 5, 1973, the world was shocked, especially the sports world. Someone had to pay! It was me.

I was "holding out" for a larger raise in 1973 since I had just completed my 5th very good season in a row for the Yankees and felt the Yankees hadn't been very sincere with the raises they offered me during that string. One example of those "raises" was a $5,000 offer after my 20 win season in 1970 that arrived at our home on New Year's Eve. I felt the "raise" was disingenuous at best, and an insult at worst. By 1973 I felt I had to take a stand, especially after the 5 successive good years.

I would liked to have teamed up with fellow starting pitcher Mel Stottlemyre and try doing a package deal like Don Drysdale and Sandy Koufax did with the Dodgers one year, but Mel was too nice of a guy, and in those days, nobody talked about what they were offered in their contracts or what they settled for. The owners managed to keep that information "off limits" to the players and to the media so no one knew what anyone else was getting paid.

I was never a trouble maker and felt uneasy about not coming to an agreement with the Yankees and our General Manager, Lee MacPhail. Lee was a really nice man and freely admitted that I did deserve more but there simply wasn't money in the budget to give me the raise I thought was fair. (After all, the New York Yankees were only the most famous sports franchise in the world and the bills had to be paid!)

Because "free agency" hadn't arrived yet, I had 3 choices as far as my 1973 contract offer was concerned: 1. I could sign it as offered; 2. The Yankees could choose to renew my 1972 contract for whatever they decided (with up to a 20% reduction if they wanted to); or 3. I could quit and never play again for the Yankees or for that matter, any other team! (You can see why the old "reserve clause" was not fair and was akin to slavery).

After I finally agreed to terms with the Yankees (because I needed the money more than ever), I joined the team and jumped back into my starting spot in the rotation. Had I been able to weather the temporary financial storm at the time, the Major League Players Association was looking for a test case to challenge the "reserve clause". I would have been that volunteer. As it turned out,

I couldn't afford to do it. Andy Messershmidt did it instead and Curt Flood finished it off a year or 2 later. Things really changed after that—big time!

I started my first game that spring shortly after our "wife swapping" situation hit the papers. The game, naturally, was against the Met's in their spring training home in St. Petersburg, Florida, 3 years since I beat the pants off of them in a spring training game on our home field in Ft. Lauderdale, Florida, a game in which I even hit a home run. (It had been the first televised game back to New York that spring in 1970. Looking back, I think that game was the most fun I ever had in baseball, whipping the World Champion New York Mets on TV for all New York to see!) Now, it was a standing room only crowd in St. Petersburg, 1973, the first time the public could be my judge and jury after what they read and heard about our personal lives from the media just a couple of days before that appearance. They voted GUILTY as the entire stadium rose to their feet and booed when my name was announced as I came up to bat in the top of the 3rd inning that day! It was a reverse "Lou Gehrig" feeling. For me, that day I "considered myself the unluckiest man on the face of the earth"; not exactly what Lou proudly proclaimed at the microphone during his last appearance at Yankee Stadium on July 4, 1939, (24 years to the day that I'd throw my first pitch for the New York Yankee's Rookie League team in Harlan, Kentucky in 1963).

It was "payback" day for Met fans and the country in general, just like what happened with O.J. the weekend of October 4th, 2008. Had the stadium in St. Petersburg been enclosed, the lights might have been shaken loose from the boos they dropped on me. The sports fans of America emptied out their closets on me the first chance they got. Whereas O.J. got his verdict read from the jury in Nevada, speaking for the nation in general, I heard mine on the field, and not just in St. Petersburg. The whole country got a shot at me, with the Red Sox fans naturally the worst, since the bullpen at Fenway is just a few feet from where the pitchers warm up. Couple that, and the fact that the Red Sox fans have continued resenting Yankee successes and tradition stemming from the 1920's when the Yankees "stole" Babe Ruth from them for $100,000. The Red Sox owner then used the money to finance a Broadway play while the Yankees went on to dominate the American League for the rest of the 20th Century, in large part due to the dominance of Babe Ruth. Historic Yankee Stadium was called "the house that Ruth built". And it was. (I had the privilege of being the last starting pitcher for the Yankees in that original "house that Ruth built" on the last day of the season in 1973).

I was forced to deal with the public from that day in St. Petersburg on. I didn't resent their reaction because I would have done the same thing; i.e. the booing etc...My new wife was a different story though. It took its toll on her when a female writer by the name of Shelia Moran befriended her in the stands one night then turned around and wrote an embarrassing piece about her the next day titled "The All American Girl" or something like that in a New York newspaper.

The fan mail Mike and I got that spring was surprisingly positive, like 95%. People wrote that they wished they had the courage to do what we did etc... In a way, I wish we would have kept the fan mail, but none of what we did was for show so we weren't collecting memorabilia or anything. What we did just happened and we wanted to move on and get it behind us as quickly as possible! (It still isn't behind us)!

Since the day after our situation appeared in the media in 1973, my new wife and I have never spoken about it publicly. We just try to live our lives, helping our immediate family, making ends meet and staying out of the public eye. We just want to live as normally as possible, like regular people, if there is such a thing.

O.J. and I had other things in common other than being found guilty. We had the same sports agent, Chuck Barnes, for a couple of years. In those days, however, agents were kept at arms length from baseball since the owners knew what would happen if they let them in (which eventually happened). Mr. Barnes tragically drowned in the late 1990's. We also had the same golf instructor whose name I don't recall since I took my only lesson from him on a cruise in 1994 where we discussed O.J.'s fondness for golf and us having had the same agent.

The other thing we shared was the fact that we were both in jail one time on the same night! O.J. was in a jail in LA after he was accused of the murders and I was in a Cook County jail in the Chicagoland area for a DUI (driving under the influence) charge the night of the 1995 Super Bowl game. I remember my jail time quite well. I had one or 2 Lite beers too many after work one night with a few of my friends when my car slid off a snowy road on the way home. I was trying to push my car back onto the road about 3:00 a.m. when I saw some headlights come up from behind me. The "help" ended up being a deputy Sheriff and instead of helping me get out of the snow, he ended up giving me a room for the night at the Cook County Sheriff's Department. The room was a cell of my own, with no window, until my wife arrived a few hours later to bail me out!

I did remember being very thankful that I'd be getting out of jail in a few hours, but in O.J.'s case he could have been in for the rest of his life due to the severity of the charges. I was also happy that I didn't get into an accident and hurt anyone, not that there's anything to be happy about concerning driving and drinking, but it could have been much worse.

My new wife did something that night (early a.m. hour) I'll never forget. I had thought that she would have been very upset at having to come halfway to Chicago to bail me out of jail but instead, brought a camera with her and took a picture of me coming out of the Cook County Sheriff's Dept. building carrying my Cook County "prisoner kit" (a large manila envelope holding my 4 or 5 tickets). We had the picture framed to remind us of the seriousness of drinking and driving!

She said that the officer who was in charge of me that early morning said I was the "Nicest prisoner they've ever had in that cell". Whoopee!

Not wanting to cause any problems I pled guilty to the charges against me although they weren't exactly accurate. I also realized that everyone is guilty of some sin no matter if it was a big one or a little one and because of that, we have, in essence all broken God's law to some degree or other. Since we're all "guilty" of something, we all need a lawyer, or someone to help us out in front of the "Judge". When I was a Catholic, that "someone" was the priest, who acted as the mediator for me to make things right with God if we did what he suggested. We all want justice in the long run and hearing the priest say that I was "forgiven" was very comforting.

I remember in the early 1980's telling a neighbor of ours in Cary, Illinois, that I had heard that John Wayne Gacy had become a "born again" Christian, and that he would be going to Heaven. I wasn't a Catholic at that time (having been booted out of the Church because of my divorce) but told our Catholic neighbor my feelings about Gacy; that anyone who truly believed in Jesus and accepted Him as their Lord and Saviour would go directly to Heaven when they died, with no need to "pass go" or anything else. She was outraged! She said, "That's not fair"!

What is fair? Who "makes it" (to Heaven)? What is the dividing line? Is faith a "gift" and is it from God or do we earn it? Why should I "get the gift" and not my neighbor, or visa versa? If we have to persevere to the "end" (of our earthly lives), how much persevering is enough—where's the dividing line between enough and not quite enough?

I thought I had the answers in 1976 when I "accepted" Jesus as my personal Lord and Saviour every night for a month until my friend and teammate, Danny Thompson, on the Texas Rangers showed me in the Bible that if I did it once, and meant it, that I was "saved" forever! I did, so I was!

I thought so, anyway.

In 2006, however, I bought a book about called "The Believer's Conditional Security: Eternal Security Refuted". I didn't understand why the author said "conditional" since I had been taught that once saved, always saved (OSAS), like most of the great preachers of our day proclaim (i.e. Charles Stanley, Chuck Swindall etc. etc.). The book scared the daylights out of me since it pointed out many places in the Bible where certain types of people (i.e. drunkards, gluttons, liars, adulterers, etc...) wouldn't inherit the Kingdom of Heaven. He then went on to "prove" that several "born again" believers in the Bible did, in fact, lose their salvation. Judas Iscariot, the apostle who identified Jesus in a crowd for the Roman soldiers to arrest, is just one of the examples the author cited in the book.

Knowing I had been drunk at least once 'on the record' since my "conversion" in 1976, did that mean that I now was teetering on the "saved/unsaved" pendulum? Do I have to go live in a church until my last breath to guarantee I was still going to Heaven? But then what if I get an impure thought during that time, during my church confinement? Might that tilt the scales backward, precluding me from going to Heaven?

With my "salvation" at stake, and with active prostate cancer working its way around my body, I decided to get serious about the eternal life or eternal damnation scenarios.

I decided that I needed to talk to my pastor about whether a person could lose his or her salvation after they had "obtained" it (be "accepting Jesus"). Even though he didn't answer my question directly, he gave me a book which changed my life forever! After reading it, I felt like I did when I got out of the Cook County Jail back in 1995, but this time I knew I'd never be back again, unlike O.J... I found out that some of the people I thought were in Heaven weren't and some I thought would burn in hell forever wouldn't! That book, and the dozens of similar books I've read like it, along with several different translations of the Bible, including an "authentic" translation of the Bible (The Concordant Literal New Testament, translated from both the Hebrew and the Greek languages) has answered many of the questions I have had over the years as I tried to figure out the truth about God's purpose and plan for our lives and which church was actually telling the truth as God had revealed it.

The survey in Appendix III, Global Missions Statistics 2,000, was the way I thought things would turn out before my search began. It is no longer the way I believe!

Keith Morrison, of NBC News in August, 2006 wrote: "Hell is for other people! Fully three-quarters of a survey of Americans felt pretty sure they will be going to heaven when they die, while just 2 percent expected they would wind up in hell." That is very enlightening since we have bought into a theological system that implies that ultimately only 2% of humanity will be saved like the Global Missions Survey 2,000 indicates.

Since the meeting with my pastor in 2006, I have told many people about my ongoing study of Heaven and hell and God's grace. I cannot believe the response I have gotten! Like our neighbor in Cary, IL, most people, especially Evangelical Christians are very upset; angry in fact that way more people than they had planned on will be going to Heaven! Even though they should be elated, they are saying, "It's not fair! Why bother being 'good' if what you're telling me is true?"

Many of my friends and relatives feel sorry for me and some now think if I live long enough that I may have a chance of being the "anti-Christ". True "believers" should be jumping for joy concerning God's grace! They're NOT!

I no longer believe what I did in 1976 when I was "born again" or for that matter what I believed when I was confirmed a Lutheran in 1954 or what I did when I converted to Catholicism in 1964. I didn't mean to end up believing what I do now but simply wanted the TRUTH, wherever it fell. Where I am now is unbelievable, God is so GOOD, and it IS FAIR and it is so GOD!

As far as O.J.'s long term plight is concerned, I'm quite sure that unless he tosses his pride in the toilet that he will be taking a long swim in "the lake" (of fire). However, if a feeling of mine comes true, I think O.J. will see the "Light" with the help of some progressive, enlightened pastor like Carlton Pearson from Tulsa, Oklahoma, and become a "first round draft choice". He then could finally tell the whole truth to the world and to God (who obviously knows it already, even though "the glove didn't fit") for the first time and possibly become a powerful witness of God's grace along the lines of what Chuck Colson has done. It might take someone like O.J. to tell millions of people what the churches are afraid to about the grace of God and what that really means to all of us!

Even if O.J. stays in jail for many years, he could still be "free", spiritually, like the Apostle Paul was when he was behind bars numerous times. Even though I didn't pull for O.J. in any of his trials, I'm pulling for him to become a first round draft choice!

CHAPTER **7**

A New Yankee Era

With Roger Maris already gone in 1967 and Mickey Mantle retiring after the 1968 season, 1969 began a new era for the Yankees. It could have been the new "M & M Boys" era (Murcer and Munson) like the one when the original "M & M Boys" stood for Mantle and Maris during the big home run chase in 1961 when Roger ended up hitting his 61st home run on the last day of the season. But it wasn't. Instead it was called the "Horace Clarke era", standing for mediocrity at best, pathetic at worst. The "Horace Clarke era" went from 1967 to 1973, bad times for Yankee fans and players as well. I know, I was there for the whole thing!

I thought at one time that I had been with the Yankees for the longest consecutive time in a Yankee uniform without playing in a World Series game. I found out after doing some research that Horace Clarke had me beat by a few weeks. Don Mattingly would beat us both out a few years later (1982-1995) to "Donnie Baseball's" dismay. Not a great designation to be known for. It brings back memories of what my scouts had told me about signing with the Yankees. They told me that if I ever made the big club I'd be getting extra money every year from the World Series games I'd be playing in. They lied! I never got there!

The sad thing, more for Stottlemyre than any other pitcher (because he was truly a sinkerball pitcher who got most of his outs on groundballs), we never had a decent infield. To add to our woes, our leftfielder couldn't throw hard enough to keep runners from going from first to third on base hits to left field, a real no-no in professional baseball. Our starting pitchers all knew that we actually began each game trailing by an imaginary run before the first hitter even stepped into the batters box. It was all due to the fact that our defense was simply not adequate, not just at one position, but at most of them!

It was still fun being a New York Yankee despite our shortcomings even though it wasn't fun watching the Met's on the other side of town winning the "world" in 1969 while we were struggling. I hate to say it, but the Met's were a very good team and with the help of the "ever losing Cubs", became division winners and then World Series Champions that year. It was a real slap in the face to the "real" baseball fans in New York who would have to wait until 1976 to get back into the World Series!

With Bouton gone by now and Mike Kekich replacing him, Mike & I had most of our fun in the clubhouse pulling pranks on our fellow teammates. While Bouton's victims were generally outside the ballparks (i.e. Shriners, street preachers, etc.), Mike and I kept our targets inside the clubhouse.

One of my favorite targets was our gullible, hyperactive, ever talking third baseman, Jerry Kenney. Jerry filled in the gap at third base between journeymen Clete Boyer, who was a "vacuum cleaner" at third in the 1960's and Craig Nettles, a golden Glover in 1977 and 1978 who could hit home runs and field with the best of them.

Jerry Kenney got the nickname from Roy White of "Lobo". I never knew why but I did know that he never stopped talking. The only player that could audibly compete with "Lobo" was the world's first designated hitter, our Jewish first baseman, Ron Blomberg, another "motor mouth". They both should have been on Ritalin but it wasn't invented until 1980. They were both left-handed hitters and started primarily in games against right-handed pitching. On the days that they didn't play, our clubhouse sounded like a chicken coup with a loose fox in it between innings. Both of them would be running around nervously jabbering and never missing a chance to say something.

On road trips, the clubhouse attendants (clubbies) would provide a food table (spread) after the games. The reason they did it was so players could eat something in the clubhouse in case they didn't want to go out late at night and try to find a regular restaurant that was still open before going to bed for the night. Some of the clubbies really put out a good spread but the best in the league was definitely Jim Weisner's in Minnesota.

Being a starting pitcher, I'd spend 4 days on the bench and one on the mound so I'd have a lot of time to wander into the clubhouses between innings to see what was going on. One night, on a road trip to Minnesota, I found the refrigerator where the clubbie had his deviled eggs hidden and helped myself to a few of them, 8 of them to be exact. He had prepared 2 dozen for part of his post game spread that night. They were so tasty I couldn't help myself. When I got back out to the dugout, after finishing my last deviled egg, I sat down next to Jerry Kenney who was riding the bench that night and talking nonstop as usual. I finally got a word in and mentioned to him that I had found the clubbie's deviled eggs and made sure to tell him how extra good they were that night. I could see him licking his chops, waiting for the inning to end, so he could go in and sample one or 2 of them. Jerry was well aware of how good Weisner's spreads were since he ate his whole post game meal there more often than not, saving some meal money.

I went back into the clubhouse a little before the inning ended, found the clubbie and said, "Jim, you better keep an eye on your deviled eggs. Jerry Kenney found them in the refrigerator and has already eaten a bunch. You better do something or there might not be any left for the rest of us".

Sure enough, between innings Jerry came darting into the clubhouse and headed right to the refrigerator where the deviled eggs were stored. Weisner followed him into the storage room to see Jerry pick a couple of the eggs out of the container and gulp them down. Jerry was definitely "busted"! Although Weisner didn't say anything to him right then, the look he gave Jerry spoke volumes. "Lobo" was a marked man in Weisner's clubhouse for the rest of his career in the American League. Beside that, "Lobo" wasn't a big tipper anyway and after polishing off nearly a dozen of Jim's prized deviled eggs that night, Weisner had it in for Jerry. (Great deviled eggs Jim)!

Weisner took other things a little too seriously as well. Once, on a 4 day road trip in Minnesota, Joe Pepitone forgot to leave Jim a tip. The rest of the year when the Yankees came to town, Joe's equipment was hanging up in the toilet enclosure rather than in a regular locker in the clubhouse. "Lobo" wasn't the only player in Weisner's "shit house"!

That was only the beginning for "Lobo". Our first base coach, Elston Howard, the Yankee MVP catcher before becoming a bench coach for the Yankees in 1969 had done a commercial for Gulden's Mustard in the early 60's. The Yankees, at the time were in the middle of their 5 year reign of pennant winning. It was really a cool commercial which was actually filmed at his home in Teaneck, NJ. It featured Ellie and his beautiful wife Arlene in their kitchen enjoying dinner and talking about how much Gulden's Mustard had added to the quality of their meals.

I thought that Jerry should have the same opportunity Ellie had so I made up some official looking Gulden's stationery with a matching envelope and, on behalf of Guldens, made Jerry an offer he couldn't refuse.

The letter read, "Dear Mr. Kenney, Welcome to New York, we are proud to have you here as a member of the New York Yankees. We would like you to be a part of our Gulden's family by asking you to do a 1 minute commercial for us. We would like it to be shot behind home plate at Yankee Stadium on an off day within the next two months. We will pay you $5,000 to participate in our commercial. We have worked with your coach, Elston Howard, in the past which turned out to be very beneficial to him and his family. Please ask Mr. Howard about our company if you would like to and get back to us as soon as possible so we can schedule the "shoot". Sincerely Mr. ---X Y Z--------, CEO, Guldens Mustard. (Jerry's salary for the entire season was only about $9,000.)

Before I had the letter delivered to Jerry's locker I showed it to Ellie and asked him to play along. I suggested that he tell Jerry that he should even ask for more money, i.e., $9,000 or so. Ellie was a good sport and loved a good laugh and agreed to help. The next morning, with many of us silently watching from our lockers, Jerry strolled into the clubhouse with his good friend Roy White, who knew about the contents of the letter beforehand. When Jerry read the letter he got a little smile on his face and immediately headed over to coach Howard's locker to show it to him and get his advice on the matter. Ellie was perfect! Even though I didn't hear the conversation, I saw "Lobo's" head nodding a few times as Ellie told him he could even get more than Gulden's had originally offered. "Lobo" headed back to his locker with an even bigger smile on his face as he finished putting his uniform on for the game that day.

Jerry thought his boat had just come in. He had "arrived"! Jerry was a very happy camper that day and topped it off by going 3 for 4 with an RBI (run batted in) and a stolen base.

The next morning Roy White came over to my locker before Jerry got to the clubhouse and said, "Hey man, you better tell Jerry that the mustard thing wasn't real." I asked him why and Roy said, "He went to Hackensack Ford last night and ordered a new Ford

Mustang convertible"!

My locker was close to the entrance door to the clubhouse so when Jerry came in I said, "'Lobo' come over here, I've got to talk to you." I said to him, "Jerry, I hate to tell you but the mustard commercial thing was a joke". He said, abruptly, "I know", and walked away. He didn't know! He was too embarrassed to admit that the thought of him having struck gold the day before had just vanished into thin air in less than 5 seconds.

Roy White happened to be in the trainer's room when Jerry came in to make a phone call to Hackensack Ford canceling the Mustang he ordered the previous night. If Jerry didn't know before, he knew now! You win some and lose some "Lobo"!

Just because Roy could hit from both sides of the plate didn't exempt him from a prank or 2 along the way. Roy and I had come to the Yankees at about the same time period. Unfortunately it was after the winning days of the 60's were over. In the late 60's the "perks" that the winning Yankee teams had offered to them in the early 60's had more or less dried up. Roy and I both had heard about the exhibition trip the Yankees had taken to Japan in the early 60's during one of those off seasons. We also heard that Joe Pepitone, characteristically had gotten into trouble during the trip at a Geisha house--putting on an exhibition of his own in front of some of his teammates. In general, however, it sounded like a really great trip, Geisha's and all!

I didn't think it was fair that we were deprived of such perks simply because we weren't winning anymore, so I made up a fake trip to Japan on Yankee letterhead. I included enough lines for 25 names to be filled in by guys interested in going on the exotic trip to the Far East for 2 weeks during the upcoming off season. (I scheduled if for after the World Series, in case we happened to be in it. Right!)

I attached a signup sheet on a clipboard with the following information on it: "Players interested in going to Japan in October for an 8 game exhibition series against Japan's 4 top professional baseball teams please sign below. You will be given $1,000 in spending money and your travel expenses will be covered. You may bring your wife but no children. Your wife's travel expenses will also be paid by the Yankees". I had a little box after the line they signed on for the players to check off if they wanted to include their wife on the trip.

Because Roy had seen me in action with Jerry Kenney's mustard commercial I knew he would be skeptical of anything that looked fishy, especially if I had anything to do with it. I had a stewardess bring the clipboard to Roy from the back of the plane so he wouldn't see it coming or think it was something I had anything to do with. Roy took the clipboard, read it carefully and, just as I thought, looked around the plane to see if he could see me watching him.

I was watching indeed, but he didn't know it. I was peeking from between the seats way up in the front of the plane. He got a nice little smile on his face, just like Jerry Kenney had when he read his Gulden's Mustard offer in the clubhouse a couple of weeks before. Roy said something to Horace Clarke, who was sitting next to him. They both chuckled a little. Roy signed his name on the sheet and checked the box to include his wife Linda. I later found out from Horace what Roy was giggling about. He had said to Horace, "Hey man, this might be the last time I'll have a chance to go to Japan"! Roy was really excited to be going on the trip! Horace signed his name too and included his wife Hilda as well. Hilda was going to do the shopping for them since the Clarke's knew, being from St. Croix, US Virgin Islands, that items purchased over seas were "duty free". Beside that, custom made suits in Japan were cheap to begin with!

After Roy finished his career with the Yankees, he indeed did go to Japan, not as a visiting player, but as a regular roster player for one of Japan's better teams, the Tokyo Giants (the "Yankees of Japan"), in 1979 for 3 years. He hit very well for them, as Roy always did! You owe me Roy because that sign up sheet planted the seed in your mind about playing baseball in Japan. I also know you got more than the $1,000 I had offered you on my "fantasy" trip.

I didn't feel that sorry for Roy and Horace when they found out that the trip was bogus, but I did feel bad for Roy and all of our black players, especially in the early 60's because of racism. I can't even begin to imagine how Jackie Robinson or Elston Howard or any of the earlier black players felt before the 1960's. When I was in the minor leagues from 1963-1965, on road trips our bus would stop at 2 different motels. One stop was to drop off the black players at one motel and the other stop was to drop off the white guys at a different motel. The motels, of course, were in different parts of town! The thing I found very strange about the whole matter was that nobody said anything; it was just "the way it was"! The black players didn't seem to mind, so the white guys didn't either. It was just "the times"! Looking back, it was horrible and dehumanizing and I don't know how anyone could have accepted it!

The Yankee organization didn't have many black or Hispanic players but other teams like the Pirates did. I can't imagine the thoughts and the feelings involved between the black guys and the white guys when their busses made the 2 stops!

That reminds me of the way I used to feel about "saved" and "non-saved" people of any race or any other religion after I left baseball in 1977. I was very happy thinking I was on the right "side" as a "born again" Christian (since 1976). I knew a place was reserved for me in Heaven, but I felt sorry for ones on the wrong side, meaning everyone else. Somehow, it didn't seem fair that everyone else would they spend eternity in hell because they didn't believe just like I did or because they happened to be born in India or Africa, or in Boston, not in the "bible belt" of North America. But again, it just seemed like "that was the way it was" (like the motel thing)! It just seemed odd that I should get the five star motel and my neighbor would get the "no" star motel? Why should my room be better than his or visa versa? Our "owners" were paying our bill, not us!

Thank God I learned that we're all equal in God's eyes. After all, we were all created by Him in the first place. I also learned that He has provided the same means of grace for us all and that He is no "respector" of man. He is also colorblind and can understand, and speak in any language (somewhat like Santa Claus in the original "Miracle on 34th Street" movie where Chris Kringle understood what the little foreign child sitting on his lap was asking him to bring him for Christmas, then seeing how excited the child was when Santa answered him back in his own language).

I can tell you something else exciting. At the end, God's bus will only make one stop and we will all enter through the same clubhouse door. Our accommodations will even be nicer than those at the St. Moritz Hotel in New York where Mickey Mantle stayed during his last few years with the Yankees! Best of all, no tipping allowed!

CHAPTER 8

A New Era in Journalism

Rev. 21:8 "all liars shall have their part in the 'lake' which burneth with fire and brimstone: which is the second death".)

Maury Allen wrote in a column first posted on June 11, 2007 in which he claimed to have been the "middle man" in a famed "wife swap" more than 35 years ago. He was referring to me and Mike Kekich of course, when we switched families in December, 1972. Maury lied! His only involvement, if you can call it that, was that the first time Mike's wife and I rode in my car together and my wife, Marilyn, and Mike rode in his car together was from Maury's cook out/party one night at his home in Westchester, NY, to a diner in Ft. Lee after the party was over in July, 1972. That scenario was never thought of, or planned, like Maury has reported over the years. As far as Maury Allen being the "middle man", no! It could have been our clubhouse man's house or anyone else's house just as easily!

In that same column Maury said that the Peterson/Kekich coverage seemed to open a new era in journalism. He also stated that everywhere he went, for a couple of years after the media had thoroughly exploited us that people asked him about the journalistic morality of telling "the tale". Ours. A "tale" it was!

Nobody, and particularly Maury Allen, has ever told the story accurately.

I had heard that Maury's book, "All Roads Lead to October" included a chapter about our "situation". Even though I hated to, I bought a copy of the book for a penny from Amazon.com and found that indeed, the 2nd chapter was all about us. In the 10 or 11 pages about us I found 43 incorrect facts or statements (mistakes); some big, some little. The final one stated in the chapter was that my ex-wife ended up marrying a doctor, (not referring to Mike with his Mexican doctor's designation). The "doctor" turned out to be a really nice insurance man from New Jersey who Marilyn is still married to.

In a review of Maury's book by L.D. Meagher, Special to CNN. Com, on July 12, 2000, Meagher said that the book was unfocused and rambles off on tangents. He calls the tangent concerning us "chatty gossip" that is "a bit fuzzy" in the facts. Oh really!

Is "fuzzy" synonymous with lying? Bill Clinton said it "depends what you mean by lying (or 'if')". Mr. Clinton carried around a book called "The Perfection of Falsehood—How to Lie With a Straight Face". Maury didn't need a book.

Shouldn't a non-fiction writer be punished when he or she downright lies?

After our situation flooded the media for a couple of weeks in March, 1973, Maury Allen sold his neighbor, the editor of Ladies Home Journal, Dick Kaplan on the idea of doing a story on us. Since Dick had been at the party at Maury's house in July of 1972 and subsequently took us out to dinner in spring training, 1973, to see if our relationship was "real", the article itself was a foregone conclusion. (Dick Kaplan is same the person who first broke the Bill Clinton/Jennifer Flowers situation a few years later). Maury called me about the article he wanted to do about our situation and offered us each $1,000 for our cooperation. I refused. I felt like enough damage had already been done to us by all the things that had already been written about it since March 5, 1973 and didn't want to prolong it any longer, for any amount of money. Most of the information "out there" had come from the press conferences Mike and I went to at different times at the ballpark in Ft. Lauderdale a day before the big news broke.

Maury called me back after I had originally refused his offer and told me that he was going ahead with the article anyway, whether we cooperated or not. I finally decided to read over his draft to at least correct his mistakes since it was going to come out regardless, with, or without anyone's input. Maury and I met at a hotel where we went over his initial draft, item by item until I thought it was as close to what really happened as possible. I had him change 5 or 6 factual errors he had made regardless of which one of us it may have helped, one way or the other, just to make the story accurate. One of the items I had him change was the one in which Maury had stated that Marilyn had "cried for Mike" (wanting to rejoin him after we had all temporarily gone back to our spouses in the winter of 1972 to see if there was anything left to save in either one of our marriages). Marilyn never cried for anything or anyone in her life as far as I knew. Maury had just decided to add a little spice to the "tale" for its literary effect. Maury thanked me for helping him fill in some of the missing facts about our situation and we went our own ways.

Although I felt good about correcting the errors in his original draft, I also felt "used" by Maury for his gain. Maury hadn't been at our press conferences in Ft. Lauderdale, FL, because he was in St. Petersburg, FL, covering the Mets at the time. I guess he felt that Mike and I owed him something because we were both at his house in July, 1972 when we happened to drive from his house to the diner in Ft. Lee with the others spouse in our car. Yes, that happened to be the beginning of our relationships but it was totally unplanned and had nothing to do with Maury or his wonderful wife Janet, like Maury had frequently stated over the years.

The original press conference that Maury missed was attended by 5 of the regular New York Yankee beat writers. They all agreed to take a day and do it "right" and not rush their stories just to try to "out-scoop" each other. Very honorable intention guys!

After my press conference was over I called Maury Allen, on the West Coast of Florida, and another "friend", a UPI (United Press International) writer, Milton Richman, in New York to tell them what had happened. I would have done the same thing, as a courtesy, for any of the other 5 writers who didn't attend the press conferences that day since I had known them all for years. I made sure to tell Maury and Milton that the 5 writers that were at the press conference were NOT going to print anything until the second day after the press conferences in order to take some time writing their own versions of the story.

The next morning I got a call from one of the writers who was at our press conferences, Jim Ogle, to inform me that I had made 5 enemies and one friend that day. I asked him what he was talking about. Ogle said that Milton Richman had "broken the story" all over the world that day, a day before everyone else's stories were to hit the newsstands! Milton had "scooped em all", leaving me with 5 angry sports writers to deal with for the rest of the season.

After having won the Ben Epstein "Good Guy Award" in 1970 for being the most cooperative athlete in New York with the media, I got a lesson I'd never forget: sports writers have a job to do. If you happen to like them, fine, but they are NOT your friends!

When the issue of the Ladies Home Journal came out with Maury's story in it, I couldn't believe it! Not one word had been changed from the original draft that Maury and I had spent hours editing in a hotel room the month before. The first call I made after seeing the magazine was to my attorney in New Jersey who had handled my divorce from Marilyn (for a mere $10,000). He said there was nothing we could do since there was so much "out there" in the "public domain" already that I couldn't possibly trace the errors in Maury's article to justifiably place the blame on the original authors regarding the "inaccuracies" (lies). We were screwed!

The first time I saw Maury after the magazine came out was in the dugout at Yankee Stadium. I looked him in the eye, face to face and said, "Why"? He knew what I meant and said, matter-of-factly, "I lied". I said, "Thanks for telling me the truth". I meant it too. I figured he'd tell me that the editor wouldn't change it, or that it was too late to stop the original draft or something like that, but no, just that he had flat out lied. A coach, Elston Howard, overheard what Maury said and told me that he remembered the day Ralph Houk had Maury pinned against the wall in his office by his collar for a loosely written article Maury had penned for his paper, the New York Post. The article planted thoughts in the heads of some of the Yankee players insinuating that the team lacked leadership during one of the pennant drives. The article caused unrest in Houk's clubhouse, something Ralph wouldn't tolerate. It also brought to mind the time Maury violated Jim Bouton's trust by writing about Jim's ailing right shoulder after he had confided in Maury "off the record" as a "friend". The article cost Bouton his starting job for a couple of weeks and prompted the Yankees to watch Jim's every pitch from then on to see if his velocity had decreased. (Radar guns weren't being used in baseball yet). Maury and Jim haven't been friends since. I finally understood, firsthand, why Houk and Bouton felt the way they did about Maury.

Warner Brothers had been after Mike and me since 1999 to do a movie with them. When they told me that they were prepared to go ahead and use Maury's book to base the movie on, I felt that I had to make a decision fast, because I didn't want them basing their screen play on Maury's error ridden book. My immediate concern was how Maury had misrepresented the type of person my new wife was and I was willing to do whatever I could do to prevent that from happening. All I wanted was for the truth to be told, not to have some twisted "tale" made up by Maury Allen and his "fuzzy facts". Or anyone else's for that matter! In September, 2007, I signed a consulting agreement with Warner Brothers, essentially neutralizing Maury Allen's fabrications.

In Maury's book he states that he wondered who would play him in the movie, as if he were an important part of it. Since Bella Lagosi is dead, the selection of who would play Maury is fairly limited. I wonder if Bill Clinton would be available? Come to think about it, our manager, Ralph Houk did smoke cigars. (I guess that would depend on what you meant by 'smoked').

The actors who encouraged Warner Brothers on to do the movie about us were Ben Affleck and Matt Damon, along with a partner of theirs, Sean Bailey. In one of the movies they did together, "Good Will Hunting", I saw that Matt had a better throwing arm than Ben. I asked Warner Brothers to have Matt Damon play me and Ben play Mike (even though Mike actually threw harder than I did). I also asked them to have a tall, pretty woman play my new wife. To be mean, I should have asked them to have Kathy Bates play Marilyn but I didn't. (One of my favorite movies happens to be "Misery", in which Kathy Bates is as mean as they get, on the scale of a Leona Helmsley or a Hillary Clinton). Maybe Hillary could play Marilyn in the movie? They do look a little alike. By the way, Marilyn isn't mean and I never met Leona or Hillary. Whatever I know about them I have read in the newspaper. Then again, I guess I should have learned by now, just because you read something in print somewhere doesn't mean it's true.

The first time I saw Maury, face to face, since he told me he had lied to me about editing his article in the Ladies Home Journal, was at a Phil Rizzuto/Gene Michael fund raiser for a school for the blind in New Jersey in 2008. Gene Michael dragged Maury over to see me (more to taunt me) because he knew I didn't like Maury and knew I'd have done it to him if I had the chance if the shoe were on the other foot. ("Stick" had watched many of my pranks over the years and knew how I worked.) As I looked at Maury during the fundraiser I actually felt sorry for him. Even though his "tales" and "fuzzy facts" had hurt us over the years, especially my wife, I felt bad for him. He looked so weak and defenseless. Even so, if my wife had been there I think she still would have decked him, cane and all! What I saw was a nervous, lost person inside Maury's eyes. All the things he has written over the years that weren't true and all the people he has hurt telling "tales". How do you live with that? I guess we all could find things we've done to other people in the past but the written word seems to go a longer way for a longer time than the spoken word.

During our discussion at the fund raiser I told Maury that there were a number of things in his writings about us that were simply not true. I only mentioned one of them to him, the fact that Mike and I were never called in to Commissioner Bowie Kuhn's office to be reprimanded after our situation hit the papers like he had reported in his book. He acted surprised and apologetic. I didn't bother with any of the 42 other items I could have rattled off to him. I also mentioned to him that I was thinking of doing a book. Maury looked excited and gave me his card, saying he would love to work with me on my book. NOT! Neither will we be meeting in a hotel room to go over my original draft to "edit" it!

Concerning Maury's future beyond the grave, I am quite sure he will have an extended stay in the "lake of fire", and not because he's Jewish, which doesn't dictate a "dip" or a "swim". Even though he won't be able to withdraw any of the fabrications he has doled out over the years about athletes and their wives, he will no doubt bump into his writing rival, Dick Young during his rehab. (Maury had called Dick Young a "newspaper moralist despite an immoral lifestyle of his own" after Dick crucified us in print because of our "immorality"). Maybe he and Dick will even make amends before they graduate during their time in "the lake"?

Lying won't be the reason for Maury's "dip" either. Even the Apostle Peter lied when he promised the Lord he wouldn't deny Him and then did it anyway. It didn't cost Peter his "first round draft choice" status either. Peter qualified in the way that counted, in his heart. (During one of Peter's most infamous days, he denied Jesus 3 times before the rooster crowed twice, just as Jesus said he would. Peter had promised that he would never do that—he lied)!

Over the years, before our situation became public, Maury had written some really neat articles about me. Many were about my dreams. One great article was about my hockey color job in 1972 with John Sterling as my play by play man for the New York Raiders in the new WHA (World Hockey Association). Maury wrote a bunch of good stuff about me but when it came time for Maury to "cash in" on us, he really did, and continues trying to. Maybe we can cut him off at third base this time before he scores on us again. I'm referring to the movie deal. Right now it seems like we have him in a rundown between third and home, ready to make the tag! I sure hope so.

Even though Maury never threw a baseball, or fish for a living (like Peter), there is still time for him to become a "first round draft choice" like Mantle, Murcer, the Apostle Peter and me. Maury will find out how to become one--sooner or later. I really hope it is sooner for his sake. I have forgiven Maury because I have no choice. That's a good thing!

CHAPTER 9

Are Baseball Fights Real?

On a close play at home plate on June 18, 1971 in Baltimore in a game in which I was pitching, Andy Etchebarren ran over our catcher, Thurman Munson, on a bang-bang play. Thurman was actually knocked out from the collision. As he was lying on the ground behind home plate, the ball trickled out of his catcher's mitt and rolled up the bottom of his forearm until it finally fell to the ground. When the ball hit the ground, the umpire yelled, and signaled, "safe". The run scored! The official scorer ruled it an error on Munson, his only one of the 1971 season. I didn't know it at the time, but the umpire told me afterwards that if I had picked the ball up off of Thurman's arm before it hit the ground, the runner would have been called out!

My first reaction to the play was to look for our first baseman, John Ellis, and say "get him John"! John was our first baseman that night and the backup catcher for Thurman but more importantly, at the moment, he was to the Yankees what hockey teams refer to as their "enforcer". You'd never know it by his demeanor or appearance but when John got "the look" in his eyes, someone was going to "pay the piper". I often thought that if John weren't such a good baseball player that he should have been a heavyweight boxer, or an NFL linebacker, or something like that. (Al Pacino came close to depicting John's persona quite well in the movie Scarface, minus the drug issues.)

Looking at Thurman laying on the ground, unconscious, I wanted to turn the "creature" (my nickname for John) loose on Etchebarren and the rest of the Orioles for a few minutes to "get even". In reality though, it was a very legitimate play by Etchebarren and one I had dreamed about my whole life, running down a catcher at home plate. Having been a pretty good hockey player before signing with the Yankees in 1963, I knew how to deliver a painful body check to someone and had always planned on combining a body check along with a general running over of a catcher on exactly the same kind of play I had just witnessed. What pissed me off was that it was against my teammate and friend, Thurman Munson, and I wanted revenge. "Get him John"!

Since Munson was unconscious at the time, fighting was not a consideration. Thurman's life was! Despite what was going on, it sure was a nice feeling having John Ellis (#23) by my side when things got rough. Thurman regained consciousness and Ellis finished the game for him behind home plate. It was just another one of those nights to remember, for sure. I only wish I would have picked up the ball as it was rolling up Thurman's arm while he was lying there! It would have spared him his only error of the year and us a run. Maybe it would have changed the outcome of the game, who knows?

I never was a fighter but always had respect for people who were, and would "drop the gloves" (a hockey phrase used when players threw their gloves on the ice to be able to punch opponents with their fists rather than with their padded gloves) and go "at it". One of those "enforcers" was Reggie Fleming, a hero of mine when I was a Chicago Blackhawk fan. He could really duke it out when necessary. I remember being at Toots Shor's restaurant in New

York one night, close to Madison Square Garden, where the Black Hawks had just played the New York Rangers. Reggie came in and joined me at the bar at Toots Shor's after the game. He was still sweating when he got there and proudly showed me the new set of stitches he had gotten that night in his forehead while doing his job as the Black Hawks "enforcer". Reggie became a friend and to this day will still "mix it up" with anyone if he has to. I saw him recently almost go to blows with someone in a ticket line at Sportsman's Park in Chicago when a guy cut in line in front of him trying to place a bet. Although Reggie wouldn't have gotten one of his infamous five minute major penalties, the man who cut in line in front of him wouldn't have gotten his bet down for that race or any others that day. Reggie would probably deck someone in church if he had to!

Ellis and Reggie would have been a good match. Ellis would have beaten Reggie on a field but Reggie would have turned the tables if they faced off on the ice. I would never have wanted to see them go at it since they were both my friends, but definitely would pay money to see them fight if I didn't know them both personally.

John loved physical contact. He was a high school All State football player in New London, CT and would have played professional football had he been able to run a little bit faster. He did have the right temperament to play in the NFL, however. After a high school game in New London, CT one of the opposing players said something nasty about his girlfriend and John challenged the entire team to a fight. It would have been him against 40 players. John didn't care. He did the same thing in 1972 in a pub in New York called the Tittle Tattle, but this time he only challenged 5 players, all linemen for the New York Jets! They happened to be enjoying a cocktail at the same pub that night when one of them gave John a funny look. I know that one was true because I was there that night. It was scary. Thank goodness nothing happened! The bar manager, Larry McTeague, intervened for everyone's sake.

During spring training that year John and I and a few of the

Yankee players were having a good time at a pub in St. Petersburg, FL when the bouncer came up to us and told us to quiet down or leave. Nobody tells John to leave! The bouncer and John had words, most of which you wouldn't want to hear. During the "conversation" the bouncer cautioned John that he was the holder of a black belt and didn't want to use his skills on him, but would, if it were necessary. John got "the look" and proceeded to take his index finger and poke the bouncer in the cheek, hard, repeatedly until the bouncer realized that John "was different" and retreated, black belt and all behind the bar—to call the police. 6 police cars arrived to protect the black belted bouncer from John until everyone calmed down. We all left peaceably and walked back to our hotel while the police watched us depart from the bar from their cruisers. After that night, I called my insurance man and added an "Umbrella Policy" (of $1,000,000) to my personal insurance coverage in the event that I got pulled into a fight trying to help John out of some difficulty. Not that he would have needed help, and I certainly wasn't a fighter, but I would never leave him behind during an altercation of any kind. (My insurance went up $185 a year because of it)!

Being deprived of an NFL career because he lacked a little speed, John occasionally made up for some of the contact he loved at first base. Unless there was a close play coming at first base, John would sometimes take throws "on the bag" rather than stretching out for the throw and giving the base to the runner. With John standing on first base, the runner had no choice but to run into him. He loved it and never once dropped a ball during one of the collisions! I can still see Dick McAuliffe, an excellent left handed hitter for the Detroit Tigers, flying through the air in 1972 after running into John at first base on such a play. He must have flown 20 feet before hitting the dirt. He then rolled another 20 feet before coming to rest. McAuliffe didn't finish the game. John did.

Later in that game, Billy Martin, the Tigers manager and notorious scrapper himself, motioned to Ellis to "come and get him" (fight him)! Ellis laughed it off. Good thing for Martin!

Despite John's brute strength, he was just about the smartest person I ever knew. He also called the best game behind home plate that I ever experienced, even better than Thurman Munson. John was a real thinker and really studied the hitters as well as his pitchers. Thurman also was very intelligent but didn't have to put as much effort into his game as John did into his because Thurman had so much natural talent. It was more 'fun' to Thurman where it was more of a "job" to John, one that he took very seriously.

I am very surprised that John never wanted to become a manager. I've seen some great ones over the years: Ralph Houk, Dick Howser, and more recently, Lou Pinella ("Manager of the Year" in the National League in 2008). John had all the qualities they had, and more, he could back up his words! Johnny had other plans, however. Real estate. While everyone else was buying fishing and hunting magazines, John was buying expensive hardback real estate investment books which he actually understood. Through the remainder of his career John accumulated many apartment complexes in his home state of Connecticut which led him to other deals nationwide. Still, I really would have liked seeing how well he would have done as a big league manager. But I think John was above that. I'm not sure he could have put up with today's "mamby-pamby" athletes with some of their lame excuses for not giving 100% on occasion. Too bad.

One day, we were the "game of the week" on national TV at Yankee Stadium. I was pitching and John was catching. I remember a funny situation that developed during that game that we still laugh about today, especially because we had a national audience to witness it. There was a runner on second base which meant that John would flash me several signs suggesting what pitch to throw. The reason for multiple signs was so the man on second wouldn't be able to figure out what pitch John had called and then relay that information in some way to the hitter, giving the hitter the advantage.

At the time, I had 6 different pitches. #1 was the fastball, #2 was a curveball, #3 was the slider, #4 was a screwball, #5 was a palm ball, and #6 was a pitch I called "the thing" (a knuckle curve). Since most people only have 5 fingers on each hand (I did know a guy in college who had 6 functional fingers on each hand), we decided to use John's little finger for my 6th pitch. However, with the man on second, it took a lot of time to go through all my pitches until I found the one I wanted to throw. (I learned through experience that I HAD to throw the pitch I wanted to in order to be as effective as I could be on the mound. If I had any doubts, I found that the quality of that particular pitch in question might not be 100%). On this particular situation, we couldn't agree on what pitch to throw so John called time out and came to the mound to see what was wrong. He told me he called all my pitches and I didn't shake my head yes to any of them. I told him he had forgotten #3, my slider, or maybe I didn't see it come down if he had called it. He said, fine and trotted back behind home plate and proceeded to call #3. The problem came when I didn't nod my head yes when he did call it, even after all of that! John just dropped his head in disbelief and started flashing the series of signals all over again. In the meantime, I had changed my mind on which pitch to throw. It wasn't a joke and it wasn't planned. It just happened! Sometimes, in battle out there, things happen that are unexplainable. That was one of them.

From 1969 until 1971 we had a big kid from Wisconsin, Bill Burbach, a right handed pitcher on the Yankees. Bill was a great guy but didn't last too long in the big leagues because when he got in a game he lost a little off of his fastball and sometimes would have no idea where his pitches were going. One such time we were playing the Boston Red Sox who had a very talented, intimidating, huge right handed power hitter, George Scott at the plate. Burbach drilled him in the back for no apparent reason, which really pissed off "the boomer" (George Scott's nickname). If you are paying close attention to a game, you can sometimes read and anticipate a player's moves in a particular situation. After the plunking, we all felt like the "boomer" was going to charge the mound to attack Burbach for the senseless drilling. He didn't do it. Instead, he trotted to first base, staring and grumbling at Burbach all the way. When he finally got to first base Ellis was waiting. The "creature" (Ellis) said something to George and one look at Ellis was enough. George shut his mouth. Ellis had "the look" again, and George, as big and tough as he was, knew better. Problem solved! Ellis was getting a reputation.

John got traded to the Indians after the 1972 season for Graig Nettles and a couple of other guys. In 1974, I was also traded to the Indians for Chris Chamblis and a couple of other guys. Together, our trades helped put the Yankees get back to the top of their division by 1976. John and I didn't enjoy similar success as we drifting off to never-never land via the Cleveland Indians and then the Texas Rangers, neither one of us ever playing in a post season game! At least, in Cleveland, we were together again, and then in Texas too.

With the Indians, John was at it again. One time after the bars closed on a road trip to Minnesota, John, Joe Lis, and Fred Beene were walking back to the hotel after a night of "oiling" (drinking) after the bars had all closed (1:00 am in Minneapolis at the time). I had left them earlier because I was pitching the next day. John and Joe Lis (also a tough guy) were walking back to the hotel together with Beene lagging behind them a bit. 2 rough looking black guys were coming toward John and Joe Lis on the same sidewalk and instead of moving to the side to let them pass, John forced his way between them, elbowing each one of them as he passed through. One of the guys confronted Ellis (wrong thing to do) at which point Johnny punched his lights out and just like in the movies the guy slid down the brick wall of the building like Jell-O on his was down to the sidewalk. Ellis and Lis knew that trouble might be coming soon so they picked up their pace a little bit while heading back to the hotel. Fred Beene fell even further behind until Ellis and Lis stopped and looked back. They saw a swarm of black guys punching and kicking at Beene, who was then curled up on the sidewalk trying to protect himself from being stabbed. John said to Joe, "They got the Beene"! Joe proceeded to rip an antenna off of a parked car and John wrapped his "Columbo coat" around his forearm (to block any knife attacks) and they both charged back into the pile to extricate the Beene from the group that was pummeling him on the sidewalk. Joe whipped a few guys with the broken off antenna and Ellis hammered a few of them as they pulled the Beene up and out of the pile. The 3 of them then ran the rest of the way back to the hotel as fast as they could with the mob close behind them having been angered by the whipping and beating they had just gotten from Lis and Ellis. The mob disbanded when they saw the hotel security guards standing in the lobby of the hotel when they arrived.

I saw Beene when he got back to the hotel. He looked a little roughed up and had lost a shoe in the fracas. At least he was alive and in pretty good shape considering what could have happened to him.

The next day at the ballpark in Bloomington, Minnesota, our manager, Ken Aspromonte, called a team meeting and cautioned everyone to not go out alone after the game that night. The "locals" were furious after their whipping the night before and were looking for revenge. We all ate in the clubhouse that night after the game! Minnesota had the best clubhouse man anyway and his food was out of this world!

John's "Columbo coat" would come in handy again later that season year at a hotel in Detroit on another road trip. John was enjoying a cocktail at the hotel bar after a game when a couple of smart aleck drinkers at the bar sitting next to him started razzing him about something, his raincoat or something dumb (bad move). After John had a few words with the unruly patrons, one of them put his cigarette out in John's martini. John then proceeded to "put out" the mans friend, then the man, before slipping on his now famous

"Columbo coat" as he disappeared around the corner to an open elevator, never to be seen again by the disorderly patrons, or the police, who showed up a few minutes later looking for the guy in the Columbo coat who cleared the bar. (Having been in few bar fights in his life, John knew that it usually wasn't the opponent in a bar that could do the most damage to him; it was the friend of the opponent. That's why John hit the friend first, then the guy who put out his cigarette in John's martini). One punch for each was sufficient.

John didn't need his "Columbo coat" for a TKO (technical knock out) he garnered on the field in Texas a few weeks later when Lenny Randle tried to run down Cleveland Indian pitcher, Milt Wilcox, on a play at first base after Milt had thrown a pitch behind Lenny's head. You don't have to ask Lenny again about John Ellis. Johnny protects his teammates and Lenny learned it the hard way, at the end of Ellis's fist. (Lenny finally did win a fight a couple years later when he beat up his manager, Frank Luchessi, then a senior citizen, after a misunderstanding between Lenny and Luchessi one night at the ballpark.)

The week after Lenny had been on the losing end of a bout with Ellis in Texas, the two teams went at it again, this time in Cleveland, on June 4, 1974. I was the starting pitcher that night, "beer night". It turned out to be the last "beer night" Cleveland ever had. With fans oiling up (drinking), at a record pace the minute the gates opened in Municipal Stadium at 10 cents a beer, it didn't take much to ignite the stadium to an all time carnival atmosphere before the show on the field was over that night. The Rangers, then managed by the man that had challenged Ellis to a fight in Detroit when he managed the Tigers, Billy Martin, and the Cleveland Indians got into a bench clearing brawl after a series of events unfolded during the game that night. I ended up watching the end of the game from home on TV after leaving the Stadium trailing by 4 runs and having a bad case of the flu. During the melee, Ellis circled the field, taking on as many Texas Ranger players as he could find, until he finally stopped when a little old Ranger coach said "not me, John" after he realized that John had him in his sights. Most baseball "fights" are nothing but fluff. When Ellis was involved, they were "real"! With John's growing reputation, players would automatically look for him if a fight broke out and would quickly go the other way to avoid him.

The "beer night" game in Cleveland, in which I was the starting pitcher, ended up with the Indians having to forfeit the game to the Rangers that night, 9-0. The last game that had been forfeited in the American League before that ironically was started by Mike Kekich in a game that the Washington Senators forfeited to the Yankees 9-0 on September 30, 1971. Prior to that game, it had been 30 years since the last forfeited game in the American League. That game also involved the Washington Senators on August 8, 1941 when they hosted the Boston Red Sox. Mike and I made more headlines than the forfeited games during the season in 1973 when it was announced that we had traded wives (and families)! On top of that, we both were traded to the Cleveland Indians and then the Texas Rangers, one after the other, in that order! Odd?

John had his best years in Cleveland. It was really fun being with him there and baseball actually became fun again for a while. Cleveland was really a nice place to play, and with John having good years, it made a big difference. I even won 10 straight games there in one stretch. It was like playing summer ball again. John used to come to our house a lot and would eat us out of house and home. He'd always make my new wife angry when he'd eat most of her spaghetti sauce before dinner was half ready. She just had to learn to live with it. That was John, the "creature", and he was our friend.

John really liked BBQ chicken. One day during spring training in Arizona, I did a bunch of chicken on the grill at our apartment complex in Tucson. It was really good! What I didn't tell John was that I also mixed in a couple of pig's feet that I had picked up at the market when I was getting the chicken. I put BBQ sauce on the pig's feet and threw them on the grill along with the chicken. Eventually they looked pretty good. After John had downed 3 or 4 of my vodka & club soda's, I moved the pig's feet out to the chicken plate so he could see them. When John saw them, he had to have them; they looked somewhat like BBQ ribs, which John loved. After giving it a major league try, and after almost breaking a tooth off on the thick skin of the pig's foot, he finally gave up and went back to eating just the chicken. The next day I showed John the pig's feet he had tried to eat the day before. There were teeth marks all over the pig's feet where John tried to penetrate the skin. Again, he loved it. Those were the good old days.

A few years later, I sent John a pig's foot in the mail to his real estate office in New London, CT. He actually was terrified that someone had sent him a "voodoo curse" from Africa or something. He finally figured out it must have come from me and was very relieved. Anyway, there were no pins in it so what was there to worry about?

Ellis was traded to the Rangers after the 1975 season and was doing great there until he sustained a season ending injury sliding into 2nd base after just 11 games that season. The injury resulted in his endearing himself to the owner of the Rangers, Brad Corbett, who had never met anyone as tough as John. John refused any pain medication after the compound fracture of his ankle, even as they were resetting it. John ended up flying home to Arlington, TX with Ranger owner, Brad Corbett, after the game in Brad's private jet. The 2 have remained friends to this day. Brad has even invested in some of John's real estate syndications.

One of the favors Brad did for John was to buy me from the Indians in 1976 for $50,000 and another pitcher. To get me to Texas to be with him again, John told me to write a letter to Brad, on Yankee stationery, saying I wanted to come to the Rangers to finally have a chance at being on a pennant winner. Brad was always a big Yankee fan and really liked the letter and what John had told him about me. John was waiting there at the airport when I got there, cast, crutches, and all. Unfortunately, by that time, the fun was over for me in baseball. Even with John on the team, I always felt like a stranger with the Rangers. I only lasted 3 weeks there before I tore a hole in my rotator cuff when I threw my final pitch in the big leagues on June 19, 1976. I'm sure it had a lot to do with the fact that I had taken about 150 cortisone shots during my final 3 years in baseball. I felt like I had no choice. I didn't have a long term contract and had to do what I had to do to stay in the game, especially since I was still supporting two families. I found out that cortisone was not enough to keep me in baseball any longer. I needed major surgery to have a chance to continue my career as a baseball player.

I always felt like I had let the owner of the Rangers down by not being able to produce for him. I also felt guilty on the first and the fifteenth of the month collecting my pay checks and not being any help in trying to win a pennant for them. The end of baseball was coming fast for me. It was a very lonely feeling.

John lasted a few more years until finally going full time into the real estate investment market.

My new wife and I were with John in Florida on a real estate venture when John was diagnosed with cancer and given only 6 months to live. That was in 1984. Since then, he has had one recurrence of the disease which he successfully fought off just like the first one. John has founded the Connecticut Sports Foundation Against Cancer in 1988. It has helped hundreds of cancer victims and their families fight, and cope with the effects of cancer. John asked me to be one of the ex-player/speakers on the dais in 2006 to "roast" my friend, Mel Stottlemyre, at one of John's fund raising banquets held at the Mohegan Sun Resort in Connecticut each year. Even though I somewhat "bombed out" during my little presentation, John said something that was a "typical John" up there at the microphone when he introduced me. He introduced me as the "Greatest Yankee lefthander ever"! Sitting up on the dais next to me was the "real" greatest lefthander ever, Whitey Ford. I was embarrassed, John wasn't. That's John, he doesn't give a shit. John is John! Our friendship overrode the facts! (I did end up having the best ERA of any pitcher in Yankee Stadium history with a 2.52 era with Whitey coming in second with a 2.55 era. John didn't know it then since it was only just announced at the last game in the original Yankee Stadium in September, 2008!)

Some people are tough on the outside but have big hearts inside. John is one of those. You won't catch him in a church or going to a prayer meeting even though he was brought up Catholic. He has been a survivor all his life and the way I read his future beyond the grave is that he is one of those "first round draft choices" that will surprise a lot of people when he shows up at the pearly gates at "show time"! He's not a talker, he's a doer. Jesus could also get angry when he had to and the Apostle Peter was a pretty good fighter too. There will be all types of people comprising the original group of "first round draft choices" when the trumpet sounds. It will be fun to see who makes the cut. I'm glad there's still time for all of us to become "first round draft choices", if we want to.

Even though the Yankees retired #23 because of Dan Mattingly, ("Donnie Baseball"), John Ellis is my #23 on the Yankees.

CHAPTER **10**

Ruth and Maris—Steroid Free!

Neither Roger Maris nor Babe Ruth ever heard the word steroid during their careers, especially the way we know the term today. The closest thing that either one of them would ever have gotten to a steroid would have been a cortisone shot somewhere in their body for tendonitis or something, not for adding distance to their fly balls. Even though the home run race between Sammy Sosa and Mark McGuire was really exciting back in 1998, it has put a dark shadow over baseball that will take years to flush out, not to mention Barry Bonds' contribution in the 2000's. When Roger, Babe, and Hank Aaron did their thing, their "thing" was real and it really meant something!

It's going to be a few more years until someone legitimate comes around to give some credibility to the home run records again. Some said it might have been A-Rod (Alex Rodriguez), until February 8th, 2009 when he admitted to having used them when he was with the Texas Rangers from 2001 to 2003, years in which his home run numbers were far ahead of his normal production. When he was "juiced up" during those 3 years, he averaged 52 home runs per year as compared to his 39.2 without "help". I'm not sure the home run record in baseball will ever fully recover. As far as a season's record is concerned, I've got to stick with Roger Maris and Babe Ruth. Roger in the 162 game season era and Babe in the old 154 game season era, both tremendous accomplishments--without cheating!

On the other hand, if I were still playing baseball and if it were not illegal, would I use steroids to prolong my career? You bet! I needed the money and I would have been willing to pay the piper later in my life to be able to provide for my family(ies) if it could have kept me in uniform a little longer! I've talked to a lot of former players my age who have said the same thing. We needed the money. I cannot imagine how life would have been had I been getting the money players receive today. A player would have to be a real idiot to ever have to work one day of his life after his baseball career is over now days. When I played (1966-1976), guys were still working during off seasons to support their family and/or to prepare for a career after their playing days were over. We had to in order to survive financially.

I met Roger Maris for the first time during my first spring training with the Yankees in 1966. It was at the hotel most of the players stayed at during spring training, the Yankee Clipper Hotel. The hotel was named after Joe DiMaggio, the "Yankee Clipper". All the players, other than Mickey Mantle and Whitey Ford stayed there, unless they had their families in Florida with them for all, or part of spring training. Roger Maris, Clete Boyer, Elston Howard, Bobby Richardson, Joe Pepitone, Tom Tresh, Jim Bouton, Mel Stottlemyre, etc. etc. It seemed like the Hall of Fame to me! I couldn't believe I was staying at the same hotel as the real New York Yankees, much less sharing the same clubhouse with them. I barely knew what they looked like and the little I did know came from watching their games over the years, on the "Game of the Week" Series hosted by Pee Wee Reese and Dizzy Dean on Saturday afternoons.

Roger was really a down to earth guy, even to a rookie "nobody" like me. I remember asking him one night what it took to get to the big leagues and stay there for a while. He told me, "Fritz, all you have to do is to have one really good year in the big leagues to establish yourself". He should know, he did, tossing in a couple of league MVP's into the mix as well! His "really good year" was, of course in 1961 when he broke Babe Ruth's single season home run mark by hitting his 61st home run on the last day of the season in the Stadium that year. Sadly enough, the commissioner of baseball, Ford Frick, announced that an asterisk would be used signifying that Roger's mark of 61 home runs was set while playing a 162 game season whereas Babe Ruth's original mark of 60 home runs was set when the teams only played a 154 game season. Even though the asterisk was never really used in any official record books, the thought of it being there did a lot to dampen Roger Maris's record setting event. He later said in an interview before the 1980 All Star game, "They acted as though I was doing something wrong, poisoning the record book or something." Roger went further and even surmised that it might have been better all along had he not broken the record or even threatened it at all! Sad!

Another sad thing for Roger was that during that home run chase between him and Mantle in 1961, Yankee fans preferred to have their "home grown" product and phenom, Mickey Mantle break Ruth's record if anyone had to do it, not someone who had come from the Kansas City Athletics in a trade only 2 years before. If the whole truth had been known, the fans didn't even want Mickey to break Babe's record! When Mickey was closing in on Babe Ruth's record in 1956, before Roger was even a Yankee, the fans were relieved when Mantle got injured and came up short with "only" 54 homers! The fans didn't want anyone touching Babe's records! Ask Hank Aaron how it felt when he got close to tying the Babe's total of 714 total home runs—no way!

Yankee fans were so accustomed to winning pennants that they thought they could even have their choice as to which Yankees should hold which records. Roger Maris was not their choice. No one was! After getting to know Roger during my rookie season in 1966 I found him to be a really nice guy, much like Mantle in a way. Small town guys with great athletic skills thrown into the biggest city in the country with some of the rudest people in the world. Many of the New Yorkers expected them to sign autographs during the middle of their meals and on the doorsteps of their apartments or hotel rooms at all hours of the day or night. Although the "big apple" made them special, it also injured them deeply.

I didn't meet Roger Maris's wife, Pat, until a dinner in New York at which Reggie Jackson served as the emcee in the early 2,000's. Everyone seemed stunned when Reggie was recognizing some of the Yankee "greats' in attendance at the banquet and came to Hank Bauer and said to the audience, "and there's Hank Bauer, the Yankee's real #9". I looked over at Pat Maris and her family at the table next to me after Reggie made that statement and saw Pat wipe a tear from her eye. Roger's number was also #9 and the dinner was in honor of him, not Hank Bauer. Rogers's wife left the dinner early to retire up to her room before the function was over. I felt horrible for her and the kids she had brought with her from N. Dakota to attend the dinner honoring her late husband and the kids' father. By the way, Reggie, the Yankees retired the "real #9", in honor of Roger Maris in 1984.

Reggie and Roger were both left handed hitters, whereas Bauer was a right handed hitter and had hit only 26 homers for his high in 1956. Reggie always had to be first. It irked him that he could never top Maris or Mantle's numbers in the home run department, not to mention Ruth and Gehrig's. Reggie was with the Yankees for only 5 seasons (due to the fact that he had a five year contract). Although he was a legitimate long ball hitter, and was exciting to watch at the plate, the Yankees had had enough of "Mr. October" and sent him packing to the California Angels after the 1981 season after he only hit 15 home runs for the Bronx Bombers. Even though the Yankees made it to the World Series in 1981, they lost to the Dodgers in 6 games. Reggie only hit 1 home run in that series. Ironically, it was Thurman Munson that named Reggie "Mr. October". The nickname was meant to be facetious but turned out to be flattering for Reggie, something that made Thuman even more angry since he did not like Reggie at all. It bothered Thurman that the fans liked Reggie's long ball hitting more than they appreciated Thurman's being the team captain. Historically, the "long ball" has always thrilled fans in baseball at home, or on the road, more than all around athletic ability. Always has, and always will. Babe Ruth made sure of that! Although Thurman was the better player, he wasn't a long ball hitter like Reggie. I really think that's the reason Thurman got his airplane; to compensate for what he felt he lacked in the popularity contest between him and Reggie on the field. We'll never really know but I've felt that way for over 30 years.

The last time I saw Roger was in an airport in Tampa Florida in the early 1980's. Roger had a beer distributorship in Tampa with Anheuser-Busch which he had been given by its owner, Gussie Busch, who also owned the Cardinals. Roger had been instrumental in helping the Cardinals win the pennant during the 2 years (1967 and 1968) he was with them. He recognized me walking through the airport and said, "Fritz, Jesus Christ, what are you doing here?" I told him I was in town for a fundraiser for a Christian TV station. He apologized for his language. That was how sensitive of a person he was! He was a nice guy who happened to have a "very good year" in a "very big town", a town too big for most people who try it out. Roger Maris was left with way too much scar tissue for the good person that he was. He deserved better!

I never knew it, because Roger didn't complain, but he had a couple of nagging injuries in 1965 and 1966 that really bothered him. The injuries caused his numbers to drop drastically his last 2 years in a Yankee uniform. I used to enjoy boasting to people back home after the 1966 season that I hit only 9 percentage points less than Roger Maris my first year as a hitter. Roger hit .233 and I hit .224. I think I may have gotten better pitches to hit than Maris did! I was an unknown, he was baseballs home run king!

Roger's last 2 years with the Yankees were indicative of where the Yankees were headed the entire time I was a Yankee. Nowhere!

40 years before Roger put on the pinstripes for the first time, another left handed hitter was putting on his first Yankee uniform. It was Babe Ruth, the man that would change all of baseball, forever! The "Babe", the "Sultan of Swat", the "Bambino", the "Bammer", whatever. All of his nicknames meant the same thing. Home runs! Whereas Roger Maris was a no nonsense guy, the Babe was the opposite. He had fun, and nothing but fun during his career. During his career he would make, and spend more money than any athlete in history, relative to his era. He would have been more fun than Bill Clinton on a road trip, if you could ever find "the Babe"!

The Babe was tailor-made for the New York market and for the Stadium they would build in 1923 and name after him, "The House That Ruth Built". The "Sultan of Swat" garnered no scar tissue from the big city during his time there. He was one of only a few people, ever, who was actually larger than the "big apple". He practically was "the apple" for many years, and in some respects, will always be the "big apple". Donald Trump would love to command the same respect that Babe got but it can never happen, even with Trump's billions. "The Donald" got to start life with a few million of his father's dollars while "The Babe" had to settle for a room in an orphanage when he was 7 years old. St. Mary's Industrial School for Boys would be his home for 12 years after his parents signed custody of him over to the Catholic missionaries who ran the school. Babe "earned" his way through life and even though he died at the age of 53, he got to live about 3 lifetimes inside those years.

I never got to meet Babe, of course, since he played his last game in a Yankee uniform 8 years before I was born, but I did meet his second wife, Claire, the lady who stuck with him to the end. I got to speak with her a few times at some of the Old Timers games she attended at Yankee Stadium in the late 1960's and early 70's before her death in 1974. Meeting her showed me the very thing that no other sports team in history can ever come close to. Yankee tradition! Babe Ruth was an enormous part of that tradition. The very Stadium I was stood in and pitched in for 8 ½ years was named after the very man she had held in her arms when he died in 1948: "The House That Ruth Built". And I got to meet, and talk to the builder's wife! What an honor!

During the season in which I had the most fun in my career, I even hit 2 home runs. After my second home run that year, 1970, one of the writers noticed that I had a few things in common with Babe Ruth. My little finger extended beyond the end of the bat handle when I was hitting, just like Babe's. I threw left handed and wrote right handed, just like he did. I ate and drank a lot like the "Bammer" and we both had big bellies. The writers began joking that I might be the reincarnation of the Babe himself. We had a lot of fun with it.

Babe was also notorious for pulling pranks on people, which I was also known for. To this day, my mind is always thinking of something I can turn into a prank involving one of my former teammates. Babe would have really appreciated the one I did in 2006 involving a Yankee great, Moose Skowron, a real solid, hardnosed first baseman who played for the Yankees in the late 1950's and early 60's and was one of Mickey Mantle's best friends.

I flew into Hartford, Connecticut, from Chicago in February, 2006, along with Moose and Hank Bauer, for a fund raising banquet for the Connecticut Sports Foundation Against Cancer organization. When we got to Hartford, a limo was waiting for us to take us to New London, CT for the banquet. We had some laughs in the limo when Moose spilled a Bloody Mary in his shoe when the limo driver drove over a curb leaving the airport.

We told baseball stories and talked about the latest operations we had gotten during the last couple of years. One of the things Moose told me was about the pace maker he had implanted during the last year to correct an irregular heart beat. His doctor had found the problem during a regular check up earlier that year. When I heard that, my mind began churning immediately, imagining how I could turn that bit of information into a prank.

During another fund raising trip a couple of weeks before the Connecticut one, I had been at the BAT (Baseball Assistance Team) dinner in New York where one of the table gifts to each of the attendees was a free pass to the Baseball Hall of Fame in Cooperstown, NY. It was placed on the table for each guest at the banquet in a plain Hall of Fame envelope, with no name on the front of it. I knew I'd have use for the envelope someday, for some bigger thing than just holding a Hall of Fame pass in.

After hearing about Moose's pacemaker, and now being in the possession of an unused Hall of Fame envelope, the "bigger thing" was born.

I decided the Hall of Fame should make a little money off of Moose's pacemaker! Everyone would win and Moose would even become a philanthropist, of sorts.

I wrote a letter to Moose on official stationery "from" the Hall of Fame's president, Dale Petroskey, with a simple request—Moose's pacemaker! After he passed away, of course! (See APPENDIX I at the end of the book).

The letter informed Moose that the Hall's staff had found out from the Chicago Tribune about his recent pacemaker and was very happy for Moose. It asked Moose if he would consider donating it (after he died) to the Hall of Fame. The Hall would either auction it off (to raise money) or place it in Moose's good friend, Mickey Mantle's display. The letter asked him to talk it over with his family and to get back to them ASAP to begin the process. It told him to call Dale collect if necessary. I put the letter into a larger envelope and mailed it to a friend in New York to mail from New York so it would have the right postmark on it. After all, Moose is a pretty smart guy and might have been suspicious if the letter would have had a Ft. Collins, CO postmark on it. I knew I'd be seeing Moose somewhere down the road a bit, within a year or so to see what he thought about the Hall of Fame letter requesting his pacemaker.

My wish came true sooner than I expected. It happened at a Yankee Old Timers Game in July, 2006. Moose and I and about 50 other "old timers" had been invited to the game and due to rainy weather, we spent a lot of time in the Yankee clubhouse just shooting the bull in little groups informally scattered all over the clubhouse. I had told my friend Mel Stottlemyre about the letter I had sent to Moose earlier in the season so Mel was well aware of what I was up to. Our little group included me, Moose Skowron, Mel, and Don Larsen (the pitcher who threw the only perfect game in World Series history). When I finally got a chance to say something, I asked Mel if he ever had any kind of joint replacement. I made sure Don and Moose were listening. Mel said, "No, why"? I said "I got a letter from the Hall of Fame asking me to donate my shoulder joint replacement when I died!" Before I finished my sentence, Moose came flying off his locker stool and said, "Those sons of a bitches sent me a letter too asking for my pacemaker"! Mel and I both said, "Are you kidding me—no way"! Moose was really angry and told us that he called Dale Petroskey, the President of the Hall of Fame and read him the riot act! Moose said that Dale told him he didn't send him a letter and Moose said to him "Yes you did, I've got it in front of me and it's from you!" After Moose read the letter to Dale over the phone, Dale assured him that he didn't send it to him. It was perfect! Mel got to see the end result, in person, of one of the best pranks ever. When Mel and I played together in the 60's and 70's, I used to let Mel in on most of my pranks. He loved them but was too nice of a guy to pull them on anyone. He lived, and laughed through mine! I hope there will be more he can be in on!

We both left our little group in the clubhouse at the Old Timers

Game that Saturday telling Moose we couldn't believe somebody would do that to him! "Somebody" did, and that "somebody" has 5 or 6 more unused envelopes from various baseball related organizations just waiting for the right guy at the right time. It's fun, a little like "Candid Camera" of old. A "major league" Candid Camera!

I have given Mel Stottlemyre and Sparky Lyle lifetime amnesty from my pranks and Ron Blomberg is covered until 2010 from any attacks. Everyone else is a viable candidate for a "hit" someday. If I can stay alive long enough there should be enough of these to fill a book. Life is too short. You've got to have some fun. Babe had fun and I am having fun again after a 30 year sabbatical! Like Michael Jordon said one time after coming out of retirement, "I'm back"! Well, I am back! Alumni beware!

Someone once asked Babe in 1930 why he felt like he deserved more money than the President of the United States, Herbert Hoover. Hoover was getting paid $75,000 a year and the Babe had just gotten an $80,000 contract. Babe said, "Because I had a better year than he did"! He went on to say "How many home runs did he hit last year"?

It's a good thing for Babe that in his day writers turned the other way when it came to ball player's off the field "indiscretions". Even though his first wife, Helen Woodford left him because of his affairs, his second wife, Claire Hodgson stayed with him despite his wanderings. Since our wife swapping "situation" unfolded in 1973, players and their wives have become fair game for the media, especially their off the field activities.

Ask A. Rod about the New York journalists! I'm sorry for the part that we played in turning these writers loose to ravage the personal lives of athletes and their families! It was Jim Bouton's book, "Ball Four" that broke the seal in sports but we were the ones that actually opened up the flood gates!

In reading books about Babe Ruth, I found that it really broke his heart that he didn't ever get a chance to manage in the big leagues. It seemed like it was one excuse after the other from owners always ending in the same story for Babe. No job! I know how he felt. I think I would have been a very good color commentator for the Yankees. Bobby Murcer was a great color man for years and I think I would have done the same kind of job he did, if not better. The one year I had a chance, Gene Michael, a friend and a teammate from the past and the Yankee General Manager at the time asked George Steinbrenner about the possibility of me becoming the Yankee color man. George said, "we couldn't do that", inferring that because of my divorce and remarriage that I wouldn't be a good example for Yankee fans. Right! OK George!

Both Mickey Mantle and Babe Ruth knew what it felt like to be thrown to the wolves after they couldn't knock in any more runs. Had they been paid the way players today are being paid, they wouldn't have needed any help. But they weren't. In both cases, they needed help since neither one had prepared for the "real world". Although they had both made that world better for the New York Yankees and their fans, they themselves were out in the "cold". Alone! Roger Maris was one of the fortunate ones but it was no thanks to the Yankees. He was at the right place at the right time, with a beer man, Gussie Bush in St. Louis.

In a way, I'm glad Babe decided to be a hitter rather than a pitcher. Had he kept pitching, I wouldn't be the all time Yankee Stadium e.r.a. (earned run average) leader. Babe most surely would have been if his arm could have taken it. He set pitching records in the World Series that weren't broken until Whitey Ford broke them in the 1960's. One of Ruth's regular season records wasn't broken, but tied, when Ron Guidry threw 9 shutouts in 1978. Babe's overall pitching e.r.a. was a mere 2.23 and his win loss record was 94-46, mostly with the Red Sox. Although he was 5-0 pitching for the Yankees, he didn't pitch 500 or more innings in Yankee Stadium to qualify him to be in the running for the all time e.r.a. leader in "the house that HE had built", historic Yankee Stadium.

Concerning eternal life, something way more important than e.r.a.'s, home runs, or steroids: Roger and Babe were both Catholics. Unfortunately, (or fortunately, whatever the case may be), what church a person belongs to or what denomination a person is a part of means nothing to God. What will determine whether either one will be a "first round draft choice" is simply if they were a believer or not. Church membership, affiliation, or involvement can be important to us as a roadmap in following God's ultimate plan for our lives, but God's grace is what ultimately gets us into Heaven, not our works or our sacrifices. What we do "for the Lord" can certainly make our lives more purposeful and meaningful, but it is not our ticket into Heaven.

If Roger and Babe believed, they will go in the first round at the "rapture" (see glossary), meeting the Lord in the air. If they did not believe, they will ultimately be reconciled to God, but only after experiencing the "second death" (see glossary)…either a "dip" or a "swim" in "the lake of fire". How long their "dip" or their "swim" will be is known only by God.

Even though their time in "the lake" might seem like an eternity to them, it won't be.

I didn't know Babe Ruth at all and never thought to ask his wife, Claire, about Babe's belief in God during the times I spoke to her. At the time, I wouldn't have cared anyway since I had no real interest in God, Heaven, or hell back then. I didn't know Roger Maris well enough to venture a guess as to where he stood with the Lord and never thought to ask his wife, Pat, when I saw her in New York at the dinner honoring Roger a few years ago. But again, at that time I didn't know what I know now about God's grace concerning everyone. I knew I was "saved" and knew where I would spend eternity but had no idea of His plan for everyone to be saved someday as well.

I truly hope they were both "first rounders" but I really don't know! What I do know is that they sure could hit home runs!

PS: Dale Petroskey is no longer the President of the Baseball Hall of Fame! Wherever you are Dale, I apologize for putting you on the spot with Moose Skowron in 2006, but I'm indebted to you for playing your part. You were innocent! By the way, the last I heard, Moose's pacemaker was chugging along just fine.

CHAPTER 11

Joe Pepitone & The Designated Hebrew

Characters? Oh my yes! These two guys both hit left handed and talked a lot but that's where the similarities ended! Pepi was one of the most talented ballplayers I ever saw. He seemed perfect at first base and just looked like a ballplayer. He also looked like a Broadway actor. Joe never lived up to his potential but he sure loved playing in games when I was pitching. I loved him being in there too because he delivered many clutch hits for the Yankees when I happened to be on the mound. Maybe the reason he liked playing when I pitched was that he knew it would be a short game, allowing him to get out to the "street" and party quicker? Joe was a blend of the "winning Yankees", (pre 1965) "the Mantle & Maris" era, and the "struggling" Yankees, the "Horace Clarke" era group that I knew only too well (1967-1974).

The designated Hebrew, Ron Blomberg, the first designated hitter in baseball (1973), was plagued with injuries during his entire career with the Yankees and later with the Chicago White Sox for a season. Where Pepi didn't fully reach his potential on the field, Ronnie never came close to reaching his! The Yankees expected big things from Ronnie, drafting him 1st in the nation during the June

Baseball Draft in 1967. When Pepitone signed in 1958, there was no draft in baseball. The Yankees thought Ron would be a Jewish prototype of Mickey Mantle in a city that is home to millions of Jewish people. When attendance at Yankee Stadium was beginning to drop for the first time in decades in the mid 1960's, the Yankees were thinking Blomberg would help them fill some empty seats and add some runs to the box scores at the same time.

Like Roger Maris, Joe Pepitone had a very distinct look about him. That was one of Roger's problems, if someone saw him, they knew it was Roger Maris and the chase would be on for autographs. Joe didn't mind the autographs but did have a "look" about him, somewhat like Fagin in the movie "Oliver Twist". Joe didn't look mean, just distinct!

Joe's other look, which was not seen by many, was unveiled after his post game shower when he was drying his hair in the locker rooms. During the time he was blowing his hair, for a few seconds he looked like Bozo the Clown. He had to dry his hair before applying the glue for his hairpiece after each game. It was very hard not to chuckle when we saw him drying his hair because the hair on both sides of his head would stick out just like the famous clown, Bozo. If I had come up to the Yankees either with, or before Joe, I guarantee his nickname would have been Bozo, Bose, Bo, or something similar, referring to his hair predicament. Since he was older than me and had gotten to the big club 4 years before me, I gave him professional courtesy and let it alone, except for an occasional smile when he was teasing his "Bozo", prepping it for the piece. Joe had 2 hair pieces, a "game piece" (which would fit under his Yankee cap) and his "real world" piece. The "real world" piece approached tidal wave proportions in height, but with Joe's big head, it looked pretty natural. The head and the hair piece together were so huge, unless you knew, you'd never guess he wore a hair piece. Maybe Donald Trump should try one of Joe's old "real world" pieces? He'd have to lighten up the color quite a bit though. Regardless, it would be better than the one he wears now. I'd like to see Donald's "Bozo"!

One of the first pranks I did on the record (reported in Jim Bouton's book, "Ball Four") involved Joe's hair dryer. His hair dryer was the first one known to have been used in any major league clubhouse. One night, Jim Bouton and I snuck into the clubhouse during the latter part of a game at Yankee Stadium and dumped some baby powder in Pepi's hair dryer. After the game Joe went through his regular post game hair routine but this time a few players had gathered to watch. It was quite a show! The bathroom in the locker room looked like it had been fogged by the Yankee Stadium ground crew for knats or something. Joe was furious! Not so much because of the powder, but because it made him late for his date that night. He had to do the whole "Bozo show" again to get the powder out of his hair. It was hilarious! After the powder show, Joe did his hair in a different part of the clubhouse from then on. Once in a great while we'd get a glimpse of "Bozo" and couldn't help but giggle, privately if necessary, especially knowing the guy under the rug was none other than Joe Pepitone. One of a kind!

Although Joe looked like a tough guy, if a brawl broke out on the field, Joe would be nowhere to be found. He was paranoid about having his "game piece" torn off his head and having the public see his dome. In one of the fights, Joe found himself in the middle and couldn't help but being involved. I remember him yelling to his opponent, "Don't touch the piece, brother"!

One of the best stories I ever heard about Joe's hairpiece involved Pepi and one of the coolest coaches the Yankees have in their farm system, Jack Hubbard ("Hub"). Hub also works the Yankee Fantasy Camps in Tampa, Florida, twice a year. He's a blast.

Pepi had rented a Cadillac convertible (of course) during the week of a November Yankee Fantasy Camp a couple of years ago. He always got a convertible to take advantage of the wonderful weather in Tampa, Florida, during that time of the year. Joe and Hub decided to take a ride over to Clearwater Beach one night on an off night at camp to hit a couple of the hot spots on the beach. It was a beautiful night so Joe put the top down for the trip from Tampa to Clearwater, a 15 to 20 minute ride if traffic wasn't a problem. While Joe was cruising along at a good pace on the bridge between the two cities, enjoying the ride and joking around, Hub looked over at Joe while they were talking and noticed that Joe's hair piece was beginning to bob a little bit on his forehead. Joe didn't notice it moving yet so Hub, having some of the same genes I possess, saw an opportunity arise and said to Pepi, "Let's see what this baby (rental car) will do?" (Meaning let's go faster)! Joe, being a sport, proceeded to put the pedal to the metal until they hit about 65 mph (in a 45 mph zone). More importantly, Hub saw out of the corner of his eye that Joe's piece was beginning to flap wildly in the wind, but was careful not to tell Pepi about it. Then, "it" happened. Just the thing Hub was hoping for! Joe's hairpiece became airborne! It shot straight up into the air about 25 feet like a clay pigeon into the sky. Joe made a futile effort to grab the piece but his Gold Glove couldn't help him that time. It was history. The driver in the car behind Joe tried to avoid it but couldn't. It was a double hit, both the front and back tire, one after another. The black seagull (hairpiece) had died a violent, but amusing death, even if Hub was the only one laughing.

Pepi borrowed Hub's Yankee cap for the remainder of the evening hoping nobody would bump into him while he was dancing at the pub, knocking it off his head. To see, and hear Hub tell the story in the clubhouse at Fantasy Camp is always a high point during the bull sessions. To know the victim, Pepi, makes it all the more humorous. Hub plus Pepi? Get ready for some laughs!

Joe is a very nice, happy go lucky person. He would have been a barrel of fun for Babe Ruth and would have fit in with Bill Clinton's escapades just as well. Sparky Lyle would make it a quartet of lefthanders nobody could beat. I wish you could pick people out of history and put them together to see how they'd get along for short periods of time.

On my first road trip from Yankee Stadium in 1966 I overheard Pepi telling the guys in the back of the bus that his new bride was expecting their first child. (The "back of the bus guys" were usually the rowdies, like Pepi, that would tell war stories of what they did the night before along with a few jokes mixed in. The front of the bus group would include guys like Bobby Richardson, a great family man and religious guy, along with the manager, the coaches, and the writers. The "front of the bus guys" pretended not to hear what the routies were saying in the back but privately enjoyed the stories—except for Bobby Richardson). While Joe was telling the guys about the baby that was coming in a couple of months he also mentioned what a great time he had on their honeymoon 3 or four months before in Puerto Rico or somewhere like that. He noticed that I seemed to be thinking about the time span between his honeymoon and the potential delivery date of their baby and he said, "Yes, Fritz, you're right, it doesn't add up. I got a head start"! In those days, people didn't have babies until at least 9 months after they had been married. Today, most of the newborns have parents with different last names. Not good! Believe it or not, my first wife and I never had "relations" before we were married! Look what happened to us after that! Maybe I should have asked Clinton what his definition of "relations" was.

Joe fit in with perfectly well with "real" entertainers just as freely as ballplayers. I say "real" entertainers because even though we were considered entertainers by the IRS, we felt like we were athletes, not "entertainers". Professional wrestlers might be entertainers, but we thought of ourselves as athletes.

The Yankees were in Washington, D.C. one weekend where Pearl Bailey was performing at the Shoreham Hotel, the same hotel where we stayed when we played the Washington Senators. Joe and I were standing in the hotel lobby one day when Joe spotted Pearl Bailey walking by. He knew her from a few such visits during road trips over the past few years. She said "Hi Joe, want to have lunch up in my room?" Joe accepted her invitation and brought me up to her room with him. It was a great experience for me at the time since it was the first time I ever got to meet a "real" entertainer. It was strange finding out that they are, for the most part, regular people. Joe was generous in that way, willing to share things with his teammates. It got me a steak sandwich that Pearl Bailey charged to her room! Thanks Joe, and thanks Pearl (who died in 1990).

Joe also likes to be funny and loves to be the "life of the party". The year before I got to the Yankees, some of the players used to wager on whose suitcase would come out of the shoot first at LaGuardia airport after a road trip when the Yankees came back home. There was generally a 5 to 10 minute wait from the time the guys got down to the baggage area and when their bags came out. All the guys in the betting pool would throw in $5 each totaling about $50 in the pot, a nice deal (in those days) for the winner. With everyone watching to see whose bag would come out first, the door of the ramp flung open and who should appear, not Santa Claus and his 7 reindeer but -- Joe Pepitone in person, head first out the shoot right onto the baggage ramp. Only Joe! The guys gave him the $50 pot for the laughs.

I always love to see Joe whenever or wherever possible. It's always interesting and fun. When I first started going to the Yankee Fantasy Camps in Tampa, Florida in 2004, Joe was the "judge" of the "kangaroo court" at the camps. The camps are composed of about 100 "campers" (guys who are Yankee fans that can usually still play baseball to some degree or another. The guys are placed on 8, 12 man teams that compete against each other during the week, playing 7 or 8 games. Each team is coached by at least 2 ex-Yankee players called "Legends". Pepi, Bloomie, and I were some of "the Legends"). During court, players are fined for such things like going up to home plate without a helmet on, or forgetting how many outs there are, or some trumped up charges either on, or off the field. The "kangaroo court" is one of the highlights of the camp for most of the guys and the "judge" has a lot to do with the amount of fun the campers have during the week. When Pepi was the judge, he was the best, especially with his personality, wit, and acting ability. Joe always had 100 guys in stitches for 20 minutes a day during court time all week. I love that guy.

On a more serious note, when Joe first came to the Yankees in 1962, Moose Skowron was the regular first baseman. Joe's friends from his hometown in Brooklyn, NY offered to help Joe move into Moose's position right away. When Joe asked them, "How?" they said "By breaking Moose's legs"! They meant it, Tanya Harding/ Nancy Kerrigan style! Joe declined. Where Tanya's husband, Jeff Gillooly was a "wanna be", Joe's friends were the "real thing". Joe earned the job legitimately in his second year after the Yankees traded Moose to the Dodgers during the off season in 1962. Rewarding the Yankees for their faith in him, Joe hit .271 with 27 HR's and 89 RBI's in 1963, his first full year as their regular first baseman. He won Gold Glove Awards three years in a row and was an All Star 3 times during the next few years. Joe could play ball!

Ron Blomberg was never on an All Star team and certainly wasn't a Gold Glove winner. I saw Ronnie drop a throw, chest high, out of his glove one day in Texas when we were playing the Texas Rangers, blowing the end of what would have been a triple play. That would have been the first triple play I had ever seen but thanks to Bloomie it was just another run of the mill double play like you see everyday! It wasn't for lack of effort on Ron's part; he just couldn't field, period! He has a famous quote out there about his commitment to giving everything he had on the field. He said, "Competing in sports has taught me that if I don't give 120%, somebody else will"! Maybe he tried too hard? Maybe that extra 20% was counterproductive?

What he couldn't do on the field, he did at the plate. The dinner plate that is, not home plate. He could really eat, and still can! I paid him $10 on an airplane one time to eat the hot peppers I got as part of one of the meals we were served. I couldn't even put the peppers close to my nose much less eat them. They burned just looking at them. Not only did Bloomie take my money, he actually enjoyed eating them!

At the real "plate", Ronnie could hit! He ended his career with a .293 batting average and a .429 batting average against Denny McLain alone. I owe Ronnie for the last win I got in historic Yankee Stadium in 1973. His home run gave me the only 2 runs I needed for my last victory there.

Ronnie was inducted into the National Jewish Sports Hall of Fame in 2004 and even though he is known mostly for his baseball talent, he received 125 basketball, and 100 football scholarship offers before he accepted a contract in 1967 to become a New York Yankee. Who knows what records he might have set had he chosen basketball or football instead of baseball?

He has a cook book at the publisher right now. I wish him luck. I think I even have a pizza recipe in it. I heard that it is now 1,000 pages long, one page for each one of Bloomers favorite dishes! I'm kidding about the number of the pages but he does have a cookbook coming out soon. He co-authored a book called "The Designated Hebrew" in 2007, about his life and his days in uniform. I bought his book on Amazon.com. but never told Ron what I paid for it (.60 cents plus shipping). He was charging players $25 a copy at Fantasy Camp in 2008, but the autograph was free. The book was entertaining, like Ron. A lot like Ron!

Ronnie is very good at getting a lot of mileage out of things. I've never seen a guy do so little in a career and get so much out of it. Reading his public relations stuff you'd think Blomberg had been the President of the United States and the Commissioner of Baseball at the same time during his 8 year term in baseball! Had the Yankees not scored three runs in the first inning of their game on April 6, 1973 against the Boston Red Sox, sending Ronnie up to the plate in the first inning and had the Red Sox gone to their 6th hitter in the bottom of the inning, Orlando Cepeda would have been the first designated hitter in baseball, not Blomberg. So, in reality, Ronnie owes Luis Tiant his spot in the Hall of Fame for giving up the 3 runs to the Yankees in the top of the first inning bringing him to the plate before Orlando Cepeda got there. Actually, since the Red Sox were the home team that day, they officially had to turn in their score card before the Yankees. That made Orlando Cepeda the first announced DH in the American League. Where it counted, however, Ronnie beat Cepeda to the plate for the recognition and honor. I am happy for him. He makes a perfect spokesman for the honor, and he's left handed! (Larry Hisle, of the Minnesota Twins, was the very first DH that year in an official game, but it was only a spring training game).

I always thought Don Larsen got a lot of mileage out of one game in a very mediocre career (the perfect game he pitched in the World Series in 1956). Bloomie was even more frugal than Larsen, getting all of his notoriety from one at-bat, a base on balls that took just 3 minutes on April 6, 1973. Good at-bat Ronnie! And it didn't even show up in the box scores as an at-bat (since it was a base on balls)! By the way, Larsen got many things presented to him after his perfect game but the one he remembers the most was from his wife, Vivian. It was a petition for divorce! It was being filed while he was on the mound pitching his historic game. While Larsen was MAKING history "on the field", he was BECOMING history in the Larsen household, "off the field" on the very same day! It was a double header for Big Don, winning one and losing one!

One thing I really thought Bloomie would do for me was to follow through with what he had promised me when we were teammates on the Yankees; name his first son Fritz, out of respect for me. He forgot! He named his son Adam, who is now an anesthesiologist! If Adam ever turns out to be my anesthesiologist I'm not going to mention what his name almost was. I may never wake up! I don't think he would have liked to be called Dr. Fritz Blomberg.

Even though Ron didn't keep his end of the bargain, I guaranteed him that if I ever have another son I will name him "Burnbaum" (my nickname for Ron) in memory of him! Abraham fathered a son (Isaac) when he was 99, why couldn't I? It might be a little tougher for me to do because of the vasectomy I had, but who knows? Had Ronnie kept his word we would have a Dr. Fritz Blomberg putting people asleep for a living. Who knows what a "Burnbaum Peterson" would be capable of if he were to surface one day?

Ronnie said in his book "The Designated Hebrew" that he felt like he was discriminated against by some of the Yankee players because he was Jewish. During my days with the Yankees I can say that was not true, at least to my knowledge. It may have seemed like it to him because he had his own set of friends outside the clubhouse and never really hung around with any of us on the team but it had nothing to do with his ethnicity. The guys that had been with me during my Yankee days weren't that way at all! I could see where a few of the 1950 or early 1960 guys might have been like that and I can see how at least a couple of the ones after I left the Yankees could have been a problem, but not my era guys from 1969—1974 while Bloomie and I were on the Yankees together. I think that one of the things that may have given the appearance of non-acceptance, of sorts, may have been because Bloomie was injured so much he didn't seem like a "regular" (player) to most of the guys. I sure felt that way when I was with the Texas Rangers in 1976 after I tore my rotator cuff and was placed on the disabled list. I remember feeling like I was a leech taking money and not contributing to the team (because of my injury). That was a horrible feeling and maybe Ronnie felt some of that because of his many trips to the disabled list. He could have misread that feeling thinking we didn't like him because he was Jewish. I don't know any player when I was there that disliked Jewish people, Hispanics, blacks, or even Norwegians (like me). We would have liked a "Martian" if he (or she, or it) could have helped us win games. I think Ronnie was filling a little space in his book with some of the statements he made in it.

His experiences in the minor leagues may have been different, I don't know, I wasn't there with him. There may have some natural jealousy playing out because he was the #1 draft choice in the nation in the 1967 June Baseball Draft. Teams in the minor leagues seem to pamper their "bonus babies" more than their routine, run of the mill players. Maybe Ronnie felt some of that? I don't know. While I was with Bloomer on the Yankees I never saw, or heard anything about any player thinking any less, or more of him because he was Jewish.

Being Jewish did help Ronnie get his first professional managing job in baseball in 2007, in Israel. He managed the Bet Shemesh Blue Sox in its inaugural season and finished first with a record of 29-12. It was the Israel Baseball Leagues first, and last season. Ken Holtzman also managed a team in the league but returned to the United States when the financial status of the league became a concern to him. Ronnie told me many stories about his managerial days in the Holy Land. The one about him having to hitchhike from the ballpark back to his hotel with his coach, Tony Ferarra, a few times because the Blue Sox forgot to provide transportation for them amused me. I can just see Bloomie and Tony thumbing a ride to their hotel in full uniform at midnight after a tough game. I mentioned to Ron, when he was first considering managing over in Israel that I would be interested in a job in the league as well. I asked him to put in a good word for me. He forgot! That time I was glad he forgot after I found out the conditions they had to play in over there. The last time I hitchhiked was in back in junior high school to a swimming pool in the town next to mine! Anyway, if I saw 2 male adults hitchhiking in baseball uniforms at midnight I'd be a little nervous picking them up no matter what country they were in. I'd think the circus was in town and 2 clowns had escaped!

Eternally speaking, I think both Pepitone and Blomberg will get a little "dip" in the "lake of fire". Joe isn't real serious about things and may be able to "sell" a priest here on earth on the status of his salvation but God knows the heart. Joe has gotten out of a few jams in his life because of having been a New York Yankee but God isn't a respecter of people or social status. I think that it will take a little shock for Joe to realize that the "God stuff" is "real". Remember the movie "The Three Amigo's"? There was a scene when one of the Amigo's got winged in the arm by an actual bullet, (after thinking the bandito's were only shooting blanks), exclaiming, in pain and tears, "It's real"! Joe may need a wake up call like that in order to realize that some things are serious and are for real. Salvation is one of those things.

I can just see Joe saying to God after he is turned away at the pearly gates, "Yo mama"! And God saying back, "No Joe, yo's", as He lowers Joe's gondola towards the "lake of fire" for his "dip"! Just before his gondola reaches the "lake", God stops him and says, "Speaking of your mother, she and your dad are already here and are looking forward to your arrival when you finish your rehab". Pepi is no dummy and will figure out that the things he had been taught about God by his folks as a kid were, for the most part, true. It won't take long for Joe to "graduate" and join his parents and ex-teammates, Mickey Mantle, Bobby Murcer and the other "first round draft choices".

Bloomie is a different story. I think he will get a "dip" too, and not because he is Jewish (Jesus was a Jew as well). It will be because he didn't understand God's plan of salvation enough to make the decision to accept His son as being the Saviour. In Ron's case, and everyone else's case, it won't be for torture, as Dante (Alighieri) has portrayed hell in the year, 1314, in his book "The Inferno". It will be for rehab and learning. (It will not be fun however)! Being known as the "Designated Hebrew" on earth may have given Ronnie a little recognition but won't help get him into Heaven. Having been the #1 draft choice in the June, 1967 baseball draft won't be of any help to Ronnie in getting through the gates either.

What both Ronnie and Pepi need is to become "first round draft choices" where it really matters, in God's "book of life", the one God signs.

That's the only autograph anyone ever needs and it has already been paid for!

There is still time guys!

Ronnie said in November, 2008 that I should write a book and call it "The First Starting Pitcher in Heaven". If I do end up being the first starting pitcher in Heaven, I'd love to have Blomberg be the first designated hitter in Heaven and Pepitone the first, first baseman in Heaven! Whitey Ford may have something to say when it comes time to make the starting lineup for the first game in Heaven, but Whitey has some time before his final draft status is determined. He might have to spend some time on the "disabled list" before he gets on the active "roster".

Photo Gallery

Old Timers game, 1992, the last time Fritz and Mantle were together.

Thurman Munson and Fritz discussing dinner plans on the mound.
(Photo by Michael Grossbardt)

Thurman Munson & Bobby Murcer loosen up
for batting practice before a game in 1969.
(Photo by Michael Grossbardt)

Fritz's 1954 Little League team managed by his dad, Fred. Fritz's sisters, Lynn & Christine are 2 of the cheerleaders. Fritz has the glasses on.

Hall of Fame pitcher Burt Blyleven, Henry Soles & Fritz talking about the Bible in Burt's hotel room in 1979.

Roger Maris
The last home run record holder before the "steroid era" began.
(Photo by georgebracephoto.com)

Babe Ruth
Although Roger Maris and Hank Aaron legitimately broke Babe's records,
nobody was in the Babe's league!
(Photo by georgebracephoto.com).

Whitey Ford
Suggesting that Fritz should have listened to him!
(Photo by georgebracephoto.com)

Mel Stottlemyre, Lindy McDaniel, and Fritz
combined for 40 wins over 2 seasons.
(Photo by Michael Grossbardt)

Met's Fantasy camper Howie Abrams relieves the pressure of another season blown by his NY Mets in 2007.

Legendary baseball promoter Bill Veeck and Vietnam war hero, Clebe McClary talk about overcoming life's circumstances in the dugout.

*John Ellis was more than just a baseball player. The Ellis building in the 1980's.
Ellis also started a foundation for cancer victims and their families.*

*Fritz and Joe DiMaggio visiting inside the Yankee clubhouse in 1967
during an Old Timers game.*

(Photo courtesy of (Louis Requena/MLB via Getty Images)

President Nixon, Commissioner Bowie Kuhn, and Ted Williams laughing and pointing at Peterson holding up a fish net to catch the President's first pitch.
(Photo courtesy of AP.org)

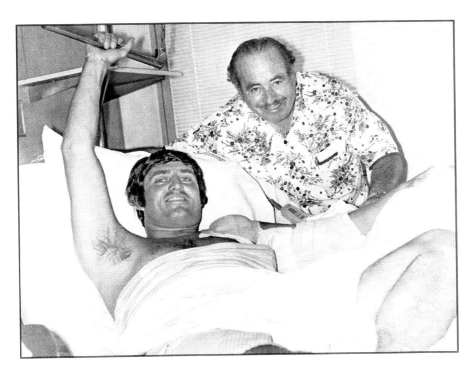

Fritz in the hospital bed after his rotator cuff surgery in October, 1976.

CHAPTER **12**

The Chairman of the Board and His Second Baseman—Bobby Richardson

Whitey Ford, in the long run, was the best pitcher the Yankees ever had. By the time I got to the Yankees, Whitey was almost finished due to circulation problems in his left shoulder. It was very upsetting watching Whitey struggle during his waning years, but it was an honor being on the same team with him and getting to know him a little bit before his career was over. Whitey retired during the 1967 season because of the arm problem after a great 16 year career, all with the Yankees.

Bobby Richardson was Whitey's full time second baseman from mid- 1957 through 1966. While Whitey was known as "the Chairman of the Board", Bobby was "the Chairman of the Word" (of God), both highly respected in their roles. My first year with the Yankees, 1966, was Bobby's last, but during that year he left me with long lasting memories of him and tons of respect for him. The respect was for his faith in God, something I didn't know much about, but watching him live his life for God and his family set an example, showing me that an athlete could be Godly and still do his job on the field at the same time. Knowing him and watching him helped me out in life in the mid 70's during a time in my life when

I was searching for more out of life but couldn't find it, even after switching wives and starting over.

Whitey was born in New York City in 1928, just before the Great Depression. Maybe that's why he was so stingy with the runs he gave up during his career. That career started with a bang when he was first brought up to the Yankee big club in July, 1950 where he won his first 9 games before losing one. He spent 1951 and 1952 in the U.S. Army during the Korean War, but made up for lost time during the next 14 years after his return to the Yankees. (The Army actually wanted Whitey to pitch 3 times a week for them, not knowing that "real" starting pitchers need at least 3 days to rest between starts!) He earned the nickname, the "chairman of the board" over the years and was also known as "slick" due to his craftiness on the mound. That craftiness included having his catcher, Elston Howard, scrape the ball in the dirt between pitches while pretending to lose his balance, or on occasion, cutting a ball with his shin guard before tossing it out to Whitey. Whitey would rub the ball in his hands out on the mound once in a while; cutting it on one side with a ring he had custom made for himself. He paid a friend $100 to weld a small part of a wood file onto the underside of a ring that he wore on his right hand during "special" games. (A baseball with a scuff or dirt on one side will sink if the ball is held with the doctored part on the top side, especially if it is thrown by someone "slick" like Whitey Ford). I only did something to a ball one time. That was when Pedro Ramos, a Cuban relief pitcher on the Yankees showed me how to throw a spit ball before a game against the Minnesota Twins. I threw the "spitter" for Pedro, but decided it wasn't for me. It didn't bother me that it was illegal, but because it didn't work for me like it did for Pedro. I also thought it might hurt my arm in the long run. I never saw Whitey throw a "spitter" while I was his teammate but I knew he was the inventor of what was known as the "gunk ball". It was a combination of baby oil, resin, and turpentine. He never showed me his "gunker". Maybe it was because Whitey was struggling when

I was there, leaving little time for the "fancy stuff". But there was no question, Whitey was slick!

Whitey did confess to throwing 2 "spitballs" during his career but also later disclosed the fact that he must have used several pounds of mud over the years to load up many of the baseballs he delivered to home plate. He was caught with his ring one time in New York playing against the Cleveland Indians. Their manager, Alvin Dark, who looked for "cheaters", brought several of the foul balls that had rolled into the Indian dugout during the game out to home plate umpire, Hank Soar, to show him the scuffs Whitey had put on the baseballs. While the umpires and the managers were discussing the problem in front of the mound, Whitey was taking the ring off and sliding it into his back pocket to hide. Between innings he brought it into the clubhouse and stored it in the trainer's room. Alvin Dark also accused me one night in Cleveland of throwing an "emery ball", trying to upset me. It didn't. I didn't even know what an "emery ball" was and continued pitching a shutout against his Indians that night. Nice try Alvin.

Whitey was such a good pitcher that he got away with a lot. I remember some of the great match ups he had with the Chicago White Sox pitching ace, lefty, Billy Pierce. Billy could throw bullets whereas Whitey was a finesse pitcher. At the end of the day, however, Whitey and the powerful Yankees would usually come out on top. I hated Whitey in those days!

When Whitey first came up in 1950 with the Yankees, he wore #19. That was the same number Billy Pierce wore. When I first came up with the Yankees in 1966, my first # was 52. The number I really wanted, #19, was being worn by one of our right handed pitchers, Bob Friend. I got #19 in my second year after Friend retired following the 1966 season. The reason I liked #19 was because Billy Pierce had been my favorite pitcher as a kid when I was a White Sox fan. When Whitey came back to the Yankees after his 2 years in the service, he got a different number; the number he ended his career with, #16. That number was eventually retired in 1974 by the Yankees because of Whitey's illustrious career, the same year he was inducted into Baseball's Hall of Fame (in his second try). Believe it or not, Whitey never pitched a no-hitter! He did, however, pitch 2 one hitters in a row, tying a major league record. I never pitched a no hitter or even a one hitter, but I did throw 5 two hitters in my career before my arm died in 1976.

During my first spring training with the Yankees, I was in awe of my new teammates, the New York Yankees. I couldn't believe I was in the same clubhouse as them, much less being on the mound for them every 5th day. Johnny Keene was my manager that year after having finished out of the money in 1965 for the first time in 5 years. Johnny wasn't a favorite with the Yankee "regulars" but he was to me. I didn't know Yogi Berra or Ralph Houk the way the "regulars" did, but Johnny was the one that gave me a chance to pitch in my first spring with the Yankees and I really appreciated it.

By the time spring training was almost over in 1966, it looked like I had a chance to make the team. We were in Sarasota, Florida for a game against my old favorites, the Chicago White Sox, late in March and I was scheduled to be the starting pitcher. Whitey came up to me before the game in the clubhouse and said, "Hey kid, I hate to tell you this, but this is it". He meant that if I did well that day I'd make the team. If I didn't, well, you know, have a good life. I think he was kidding because he was in the "in group" and probably knew I had already "made it". I don't know. I went the 6 innings the Yankees had me scheduled for and beat the White Sox. I gave up just one run, a home run to Tommy Agee in the 5th inning. I had made the team! I never did ask Whitey if he had known ahead of time that I actually had made the team. I guess I didn't care; I was just elated to be a New York Yankee. As it turned out, I actually replaced Whitey as the "Yankee left-hander" for 8 years until Ron Guidry eventually replaced me in 1977. Guidry then became the "Yankee left-hander" for the next 10 seasons.

We ended spring training in Atlanta in 1966 where we played an exhibition game against the Braves in their home park. When we took off from Atlanta after the game, we had to turn around and go back to the airport because the light on the landing gear stayed on after take off. It's an FAA regulation. I thought I was going to end my career in an airplane that day, as did many of my new teammates. The landing gear was OK as the maintenance crew replaced the faulty light switch. We lived! It was New York, here we come. I had never even seen the city before, especially as a member of the famous New York Yankees. And not just as a tourist!

When we flew over New York City, it looked 10 times bigger than my home city of Chicago, the only other city I had ever seen from the air. It was both scary and exciting at the same time. After we landed, we boarded our chartered bus for the trip from LaGuardia Airport to Yankee Stadium. When we arrived at the Stadium another rookie, Dooley Womack and I walked out to the Yankee dugout and then strolled out to the monuments in center field to see what it felt like. We had seen the monuments on television before but wanted to check them out in person. They were awesome! I never dreamed at the time that I would be the starting pitcher in the last game ever to be played in that stadium (the original "house that Ruth built") 8 years later on the last day of the season in 1973!

We got off to a terrible start when the season opened two days after we had arrived in New York from Atlanta. We lost our first 3 games at Yankee Stadium, a precursor to what was about to happen that year. We were headed for a last place finish! The last time that had happened was in 1912, ten years before "the house that Ruth built" was even thought of. The Yankees weren't even called the "Yankees" at the time; they were called the New York Highlanders. In essence, in name, 1966 was the first time the "New York Yankees", per se, had EVER finished in last place! (Great year to break in as a rookie)!

I was the 4th starter at the beginning of the season and was slated to pitch the opener in Baltimore against the Orioles, a team that was starting to look very similar to the Yankee teams of old. They had just picked up Frank Robinson during the off season and were becoming a powerhouse for the next few years. The O's mixed great pitching with a powerful offense and an impeccable defense. For the next 8 years I watched them and tried to imagine what it would have been like to pitch on a team that had great defense and great offense. We had neither the whole time I was a Yankee. I felt even worse for Mel Stottlemyre, my buddy, who would have been a Hall of Famer had he either been on the Orioles during those years or with the Yankees of the 50's and early 60's. We were both born 10 years too late! (For the record, Mel is 2 months older than I am). Come to think of it, if we had been born 10 years before we actually were, we'd be 10 years older now. If that weren't bad enough, the types of cancer that Mel and I have had in the past 10 years probably would have killed both of us by now! (It is quite clear that the advances in cancer research during the last 10 years saved both of us, for now anyway). I'm glad to be my real age, as is Mel. So what if it did cost us a few World Series rings and Mel a spot in Cooperstown! At least Mel got his first World Series ring in 1964 and I got my dream wife in 1974 because were we on the Yankees when we were! Mel still has his ring and I still have my new wife, and, we're both still alive!

In starting the opening game on the road in 1966, I never envisioned what it would feel like going out to the mound with 44,000 people rooting against me! The vision became real when the first hitter I faced got a hit and ended up scoring before the inning was over. It was my initiation into the big leagues. The hitter was the Orioles lead off man, Luis Aparicio, one of my favorite players back when I was a Chicago White Sox fan just 4 years before. The good news was that the Orioles didn't score again until the 9th inning when Frank Robinson hit his first home run as an American Leaguer making the score 3-2 Yankees. The next hitter, Boog Powell, a huge left handed hitter, grounded out to second for the last out! We won! I was hoping, and really thought my new teammates might carry me off the field like they do in the movies. After all, first win of the season for the Yankees, my first big league win, a complete game, etc. etc... To them, however, it was business as usual. No big deal. To me it was a very big deal! I didn't sleep all night! I was finally a New York Yankee and officially in the record books!

Our pitching coach, Jim Turner, wanted me to throw my curveball like Whitey did. I tried, but couldn't. Everyone is different and needs to do what 'they' can do, not what someone "else" does. Besides, I never knew about all the stuff Whitey used to load his baseballs up with out on the mound. I'm not even sure our pitching coach knew what Whitey was putting on the baseballs to make them do tricks. (With all that foreign stuff on the baseballs Whitey threw, his curveball might have thrown itself, similar to some of today's weighted bowling balls). By fiddling with my curveball, my pitching coach actually set me back a bit. It was not intentional, of course, but I think that most coaches' say too much to players, often trying to justify their jobs, whatever those jobs might be (pitching coach, hitting coach, etc.). I think the less said the better at the major league level. Jim Turner was a wonderful and sincere man and I tried to honor him by listening to everything he said. In the long run, however, I did what I had to do, and did it without offending the "Colonel" (Jim Turner). The way I did it was by thanking him for helping me (although he usually didn't) and moving on, doing it my way but letting him think it was his. While Jim Bouton and Mike Kekich would disagree verbally with our pitching coach, I wouldn't. I just said thanks and went on. They preferred arguing and the Yankees preferred trading them, Bouton in 1968 and Kekich in 1973.

Whitey was given an honorary pitching coaches job, of sorts, in 1967. He handled it very nicely, saying very little to us about pitching, not wanting to step on Jim Turners toes. Mel and I didn't need any help out there anyway, except on the field, which we didn't get. We knew what we had to do: hold our opponents to 1 run and pitch 9 innings! Even with that, I lost 2 games in 1967, 1-0. I don't know how many times it happened to Mel. I still get tired thinking about how hard pitching was during those years for the Yankees. In retrospect, however, I wouldn't trade losing as a Yankee for winning as Tampa Bay Ray, or worse yet, a New York Met! The Yankees are the Yankees. Have you ever seen a movie called, "The Pride of the Devil Rays", or worse, "The Pride of the Mets"? I don't think so. The Three Stooges and the Marx Brothers are all dead. There would be nobody to play the parts of the players in those movies!

The Bronx Bombers continued struggling until they had finally had enough of Johnny Keene and fired him during our first trip to California in 1966. It was only his second season as the Yankee manager. We had won only 4 games out of our first 20, and 2 or those wins were mine. Ralph Houk replaced Johnny Keane in May, 1966 but by then, it was too late. The Yankee skid was in full bloom. Keane died of a heart attack 9 months later in Texas while the Yankees continued dying for 9 more years in the Bronx. The "Bronx was truly burning"! They finally put back all the pieces again and won everything in 1976, long after Whitey, Mickey, Roger, Stottlemyre, Howard, Murcer, Pepitone, Tresh, Boyer, Horace Clarke, and I were gone! Only Roy White and Thurman Munson were left from our core group from 1970 to enjoy earning their first World Series rings as New York Yankees.

Whitey had surgery for a circulation problem in his left shoulder after the World Series in 1964, and once again in August of 1966. He called it quits during the 1967 season when it was evident that his arm just couldn't take it anymore. As much as Whitey would have liked to have finished his career with his greatest friend, Mickey Mantle, there was no way that Whitey could have pitched another year and a half until Mickey finally bowed out after the 1968 season. It was sad seeing Whitey and Mickey die (figuratively) before my very eyes as the Yankees, in general, were coming apart.

I'm sure a bunch of Yankee haters in New York and around the world were in their glory in those days but it was tough to take as a player, watching and feeling it all. It didn't help seeing the "Amazing Mets" strutting around town and then actually winning the "world" in 1969, only a year after Mantle had retired. (The Chicago Cubs had handed the Mets the pennant in 1969 after having had a 10 game lead in August, only to crash, finishing 8 games behind the Mets by the time the season was over at the end of September. That was the season that Ron Santo jumped up and clicked his heals after every Cub home victory. The clicking stopped on August 28, 1969)! All in all, I wouldn't have gone to a Met's game if you paid me back then. I still won't go to a Mets game. I'll go to a circus with the grand kids instead, thank you! At least Ringling Brothers has tradition behind them.

Whitey's best year had to be in 1961 when he won the Cy Young Award and was the World Series MVP. Because of the highly publicized home run race between the M & M Boys (Mantle and Maris) Whitey's record was hardly even noticed that season. Pitchers are rarely idolized the way power hitters are. (While Mickey and Roger were pounding out home runs at a record clip, Whitey was quietly getting ground ball after ground ball and racking up win after win until he had accumulated 25 during the regular season). The only exception for pitchers might be when they can throw 100 mph or more like Sandy Koufax, Nolan Ryan, or Roger Clemens. (Clemens is now known for something more than his fastball and is getting a little different kind of publicity these days than he's been used to. I hate to say it, but his "new image" will follow him wherever he goes and as long as he lives. I know about those kinds of things)! Whitey posted a season record of 25-4 and won 2 games in the World Series. The first series win was a 2 hitter and the second one was a shutout (with relief help), leading the Yankees to win yet another World Series.

At the end of the season, each player used to get a list with everyone's name, address, and phone number on it. It was a very private and guarded list. Whitey made sure to remind me after my first year that I had to be with the Yankees for 5 years before I could send any of the players Christmas cards! It was a seniority thing in those days. Now days, players are so secretive and guarded that the teams no longer give out address or phone numbers to anybody, including fellow teammates! The only entities that get access to that stuff now are: the Players Association office, Major League Baseball's office, and "Uncle Sam's" office.

1966 was the last year Bobby Richardson was Whitey's second baseman, or anyone's second baseman for that matter. Horace Clarke took over for him for the next 7 years, typifying the mediocre play on the field the Yankees would feature from 1967 through 1973. After Bobby left, that period in Yankee history became known as "The Horace Clarke era". It wasn't a good era for Yankee fans and even worse for Yankee players!

Bobby was a very steady influence on the Yankees every year he was on the team (1955-1966). Despite his lifetime average of .266, he was always a presence on the field, both offensively and defensively. Before Bobby's career was over, he was to be an All Star 8 times, a Gold Glove winner 5 times (in a row), and the MVP of the World Series in 1960, even though the Yankees were the losing team. Nobody else has ever gotten the World Series MVP Award while being a member of the losing team. The Yankees haven't had a Gold Glove Winner at second base since Richardson got his last one in 1965! Willie Randolph was good, but never good enough to win the award.

During the late 50's and early 60's the Yankees hired a private investigator to check on Bobby's teammates, namely Mickey, Whitey, and Billy Martin. They never checked Bobby's room! (There would have been more of a reason to check Mother Teresa's room than Bobby's). Where he sat on the bus ride to the ball parks from the hotels told something about his character—he sat up in the front, away from all the cussing and bad jokes. Although everyone knew he was a "religious" guy, Bobby never forced his beliefs on anyone. He never judged anyone either. The guys respected him, period. In my case, the respect went a long way, even to this very day, long after we were teammates in New York in 1966. Oddly enough, a man very opposite in lifestyle from Bobby's made it possible for him to become the starting second baseman for the Yankees and get uniform #1 in 1957, all at the same time. It was Billy Martin. It happened a month after the famous fight Martin got into at the Copacabana night club in New York City on May 16, 1957 while celebrating his 29th birthday with Mickey and Whitey. They might as well have celebrated Billy's last year as the Yankee second baseman, because it would be. Billy got traded to Kansas City as a result of the fight and, off the record, because he was such a bad influence on Mickey and Whitey. The fact that the Yankees saw that Richardson could handle Martin's second base position sealed the deal to finally get rid of Billy. Bobby Richardson was the Yankee's new second baseman and wore #1 until it was on the back of Bobby Murcer in 1969, 3 years after Richardson's retirement. Martin got it again when he came back to manage the Yankees in 1975. Murcer had been traded away to play for the Giants and then the Cubs for a few years and never got his old number back. Murcer ended his career wearing #2.

In the early 1960's the Yankees were not known for knocking down Church doors on Sunday mornings looking for a sermon or a Mass to attend on the road. They were known for winning pennants. Every Sunday, however, everyone knew their second baseman would be sitting in a pew at a Baptist Church somewhere, no matter how inconvenient it might be. The respect the players had for Bobby was unprecedented. The only other time I saw any real evidence of respect for a guy's "religious" commitment came later in my career in Cleveland when I was with the Indians. In that case, it was our catcher, Alan Ashby, a Mormon. (In those days I didn't know the difference between a Baptist and a Mormon. They all looked alike to me. I did know the difference between a Lutheran and a Catholic, however, since I was one of each of those for a few years until I eventually got booted from the Catholic Church because of my divorce. Neither affiliation helped me—at the time). It wasn't Alan's Church that the guys respected, but the person, Alan Ashby and his lifestyle. Players watch each other and if they don't "walk the talk", they get "written off" as not being credible, or real; somewhat like Elmer Gantry in the 1960 movie played by Burt Lancaster. Ashby and Richardson had earned their credibility with their teammates both at home and on the road, like the Apostles did as they watched Jesus live His life (& death).

One Sunday, during a road trip to Detroit, Bobby Richardson and Red Barber (one of the Yankee announcers, and Radio Hall of Famer) arranged for a room at the team's hotel to have a speaker come in to give a "mini sermon" for any of the players interested in attending. Since Bobby personally invited me, I went, but really didn't want to be there. 10 years later I couldn't get enough mini, or maxi "sermons"! 1966 hadn't been my time, yet! 1976 was a different story.

Bobby was one of the few players that could, and did, walk away from the Yankees without "having" to quit for one reason or another. I didn't know it at the time, but the Yankees offered Bobby Richardson a 5 year contract if he agreed to play for them for one last season in 1966. Tony Kubek had to leave baseball after the 1965 season due to his ailing back and the Yankees couldn't afford to lose both their shortstop and second baseman at the same time. (Bobby had planned on quitting after the 1965 season but agreed to play one more year to help the Yankees out. It didn't work! We still tanked!) Another player, in my era that was able to walk away from the Yankees was Jake Gibbs, the Ole Miss All American quarterback (in 1961). When Jake told Stottlemyre and me that he was retiring after the 1971 season, Mel and I both looked at each other and realized that we were jealous. Nobody walked away from the Yankees, or baseball, of their own volition! Our shoulders (Mel's right and my left) both were aching as Jake told us in the Yankee dugout that day that he was quitting after the season. We were envious because our jobs, on the mound, were very difficult in those days. We would have liked to have been in a position to be able to quit if we wanted to. Not that we would have quit, but just to have had the choice would have been nice.

Joe DiMaggio was another one who could have played again for another season in 1952 if he had wanted to, but walked away. His numbers had dropped to the point where he just wasn't "Joe DiMaggio" any longer, but just another player. Joe couldn't accept being "regular" and hung em up. Most players are traded away before they call it quits. Moose Skowran and Hank Bauer are good examples, both being farmed off to other teams at the end of their careers even though they had contributed so much to the Yankees in their hay days. Same with Elston Howard. It was very sad to see Ellie in a Red Sox uniform in 1967 & 1968! Some players quit simply because their bodies can't take it anymore. Like Mantle, Ford, & Kubek. Very few walk away like Bobby did. Today's players should be able to leave the game quite easily with the kind of money they're getting. In my era, players actually worked during off seasons to help support their families.

Bobby had a lot of things going for him after he left the Yankees. He even ran for the US Congress in South Carolina in 1976 at President Gerald Ford's urging. Bobby was defeated by the Democratic incumbent, Kenneth Holland by less than 3,000 votes. The ironic part was that his old friend, and ex- teammate, Tony Kubek, refused to campaign for Bobby because Bobby was a Republican. Tony was a Democrat. Tony had retired as Bobby's teammate in 1965 because of a bad back and as a friend in 1976 because of politics. Believe it or not, Tony and Bobby ended up with the same lifetime batting averages, .266! Kubek had 23 more home runs than Bobby in his career but neither one had been hired for his power hitting. As a double play combination they were unbeatable! Ask Whitey Ford. They were known as the "Milkshake Twins" by manager Casey Stengel because they didn't drink alcohol. Stengel also said, facetiously of Richardson, "Look at him. He doesn't drink, he doesn't smoke, he doesn't chew, he doesn't stay out late, and he still can't hit .250". (Casey couldn't add too well. Bobby hit less than .250 only twice as a regular, both of those times hitting .247 but hit over .300 during two of those 10 years)!

I'm not too proud of this one, but in 1970, during an Old Timers Day at Yankee Stadium, Casey Stengel was sitting at the picnic table, signing some baseballs in the middle of the Yankee clubhouse, when my oldest son, then 3 years old, walked up to Casey and kicked him in the shin saying, "Take a shit"! Elston Howard, then coaching for the Yankees had put him up to it. Before I knew anything about it, it was all over. Ellie did it to pay me back for all the pranks I did to him in the clubhouse over the years. I hope my son doesn't remember the incident because I surely don't remind him of it. Had it been someone else's kid I would have laughed my ass off. But not my own kid! Not to the "Old Perfessor", Casey Stengel, the Hall of Famer who hit the very first home run in a World Series game at Yankee Stadium in the first year of its existence in 1923! (Too bad that the home run Casey hit was in a New York Giant uniform)! Casey had been a big prankster in his day and I believe that the old statement, "what goes around comes around", is true. It came around, to Casey's shin at the ripe old age of 80, the same year the Yankees retired his number (37)!

Bobby Richardson envisioned a day when ballplayers could attend a worship service at the ballpark if they wanted to on Sundays before a game.

An ex-drunk and sportswriter in Detroit, Watson Spoelstra (Waddy), made Bobby's dream come true in 1974. Waddy persuaded Baseball Commissioner, Bowie Kuhn, to let Baseball

Chapel Inc. put a worship program together providing speakers at all the major league ballparks on Sunday mornings for short, 15 minute mini sermons, of sorts. Kuhn agreed, and actually funded the original program with $5,000 from Major League Baseball's coffers! The year before that, Mr. Kuhn publicly called my marital situation "deplorable". Maybe he thought a few sermons would prevent a situation like mine from happening again? (The Commissioner had been prodded by a prominent New York Times sports writer, Joe Durso, to make some kind of statement after our wife swapping situation had become public in March, 1973. Kuhn had never intended to make any public statement about our private lives until Joe pressured him into making one. Thanks Joe! Joe died on December 31, 2004. I always thought Joe was a friend).

Ironically, I ended up being the "Player Coordinator" for Baseball Chapel in 1979, working with the most wonderful man in the world, Waddy Spoelstra, Baseball Chapel's director and founder since its inception in 1974. Oddly enough, I was asked to give the "mini sermon" at the Playoff Chapel service in Milwaukee in 1982 on behalf of Baseball Chapel. I delivered my message to the media at their luncheon before the game. The message that day was, "If I could be saved, anyone could be"! Commissioner Bowie Kuhn introduced me at the dais! By then he had forgotten how "deplorable" my situation was. Mr. Kuhn died on March 15, 2007 in Pointe Vedra Beach, Florida. He had moved to Florida to protect his house and other assets from bankruptcy. Mr. Kuhn never guessed that he would be elected into the Baseball Hall of Fame in 2008. I always thought he was a decent guy.

Waddy "voluntarily" stepped down from his leadership position with Baseball Chapel in 1983 after one of the original Chapel board members that he had appointed sent the Commissioner of Baseball a letter insinuating that Waddy was becoming senile! Not! (I quickly learned about human egos in ministries, and later saw the same things happen in some churches)! I resigned from Baseball Chapel when Waddy turned in his "resignation". He was NOT senile! Bobby Richardson stepped in and acted as the President for Baseball Chapel for 10 years. As usual, Bobby did a great job.

Whitey Ford is a sharp guy, but he has been pampered from the day he put on a Yankee uniform in 1950, to this very day. He was even handled with kid gloves by the US Army when he was in their uniform for 2 years. Eternally speaking, it appears as though God has placed Whitey on the "disabled list" for now. Like so many people, he needs a little humility. God doesn't care about Whitey's World Series records or his winning percentages. He cares about Whitey's heart, which at this time, in my opinion, isn't too concerned about things of the Lord. It is a very difficult to be humble when people treat you like God, especially in New York. I hope Whitey can find room in his heart for God and skip the "dip". For now, however, Whitey doesn't appear to be a "first round draft choice". Maybe he can come up with a new pitch for God and get off the disabled list? I sure hope so.

Bobby Richardson is a "shoe in" as a "first round draft choice". Believe it or not, it has nothing to do with his Church attendance. There are millions of people who go to Church or Mass every day, including pastors and priests, who aren't "first round draft choices". Most think they are but the majority are just going through the motions. Kneeling, taking communion, genuflexing and all that, but in their hearts, most are "lost". They will be taking "dips" or "swims" in the "lake of fire", for one simple reason, they are not "saved" ("believers")--yet. Unfortunately, one day, everyone who is not saved will hear the worst words they will ever hear, dwarfing the feared, "You have cancer" phrase. The worst words possible will be, "Depart from Me, I never knew you"! Church attendance, tithing, or anything we "do" has nothing to do with our entrance into Heaven. It's what we believe in our hearts. Certain things will count toward our rewards in Heaven later, but not for entrance. Bobby Richardson's heart is right and he is a "true believer". He is a "first rounder draft choice". Bobby will be the first second baseman on the "All Saints" team wearing #1 in his white uniform. They will play "Lucifer's Losers" during the 1,000 year millennial game played on earth (at the new Yankee Stadium, of course)! Billy Martin will be on the visiting team wearing a red uniform and his asbestos underwear. Whether Billy gets #1 or not will depend on how long his "rehab" in the "lake" will be.

Guess who wins?

CHAPTER **13**

Vacancy at Third Base!

I started with a "real" third baseman and ended with a "real" third baseman but between the "real" guys, there was a "vacancy sign" posted at third base by the New York Yankees. In 1966 Clete Boyer was at third and in 1973 Graig Nettles eventually filled the slot but in the interim, the Yankees were hurting at third base. Clete never won a Gold Glove in the American League at third but not because he wasn't 1st rate. There was another guy in the American League named Brooks Robinson, a born Gold Glove winner that won it every year Clete was in the league! Nettles was a Gold Glove winner for the Yankees in 1977 and 1978. The guy that played there the most during my time with the Yankees was definitely not a Gold Glove winner, Jerry Kenney. Bobby Cox rented the space briefly, as did Charlie Smith, Celerino Sanchez, Rich McKinney, and a few others, but Jerry Kenney was out there most of the time in 1969, 1970, and 1971.

Jerry is a very nice guy, maybe because he grew up in the Midwest, in Beloit, Wisconsin. I grew up a couple of hours from him in the Northwest Suburbs of Chicago. We never knew each other until we met in Shelby, NC for part of the summer with the Shelby Yankees

in 1964. I don't even remember being there with Jerry in Shelby???
I do remember meeting in NewYork at Yankee Stadium in 1967,
but not in the minors. We did have one thing in common, we both
started our careers getting a hit the first time we went to the plate in
a Yankee uniform. My hit was only a single in 1966 but Jerry's was
a round tripper in 1967 during his short stint with the Yankees that
summer. He hit only 5 more the rest of his career during 6 seasons.
It was tough watching Brooks Robinson manning the hot corner for
the Baltimore Orioles then looking over my right shoulder seeing
Jerry Kenney out there for us. Again, it was just another indicator
of the state of the Yankees organization during the "Horace Clarke
era". Can you imaging what it was like being a sinkerball pitcher
with Jerry Kenney at third, Tom Tresh (or someone else) at short, and
Horace Clark at second. Do you think there was a chance for a
double play even if you did your job and got the batter to hit the ball
on the ground? Then, if the ground ball that you got the opposing
batter to hit ended up in left field, the runner who was on first base
would not hesitate running to third because your left fielder couldn't
throw the ball hard enough to beat him there! That was a snapshot
of what our pitchers had to face on a daily basis during the "Horace
Clarke era". Not fun! Poor Mel Stottlemyre, Steve Kline, and me
(sinkerball pitchers)!

During one of the off seasons, I actually wrote Lee MacPhail,
our General Manager, and asked him to please give Jerry Kenney
away to some team for Christmas. It wasn't that I didn't like Jerry, I
did. I just wanted to win one time and we weren't going to do it with
Jerry at third or Horace Clarke, who also was a very nice person, at
second. Horace couldn't turn a double play. It was very frustrating!
I was in the middle of my career, (1968-1972), having 5 very good
seasons in a row knowing we couldn't win a pennant, much less
play in a World Series. (Believe it or not, Mel only had 4 winning
seasons in a row in his great career. Whitey Ford had 14, during
better days)! Even though we came in second in 1970, we were

no match for the Baltimore Orioles. They were so good that all the other teams in the league gave up trying. We had a couple of guys having very good individual years that season which kept us closer than we would normally have been, but there still was no way we could contend with the Orioles. Nobody could that year!

Ironically, it was Jerry Kenney that drove in the 2 runs that helped make me become a 20 game winner in 1970 on the last game of the season in Boston that year. The funny part is that before the game, I asked our manager, Ralph Houk, not to start Jerry at third that night because I wanted guys in that game who I knew would take a grounder in the face for me if they had to. Jerry wouldn't have done that for me or anyone else. I wanted someone in there like John Ellis or even Curt Blefary that would, even if their lack of ability at third could have cost me the game. The game meant nothing to either team in the standings. Somehow I felt that it would be the last time I would have a chance to win 20 games in one season and didn't want to take any chances. The only 2 players that were fighting for anything special that night were me, going for my 20th win, and Carl Yazstremski, going for the batting title that year. I got my wish but Yaz fell short of his by only .0001 percentage points. (During the game, Yaz was given a base hit by the official scorer, on a ground ball that was bobbled by our shortstop. As it turned out, he needed 2 hits to win it over Alex Johnson of the California Angels. Despite the help from the official scorer, a sports writer from Boston, Yaz finished second in the league with a batting average of .329, his career high). Ralph knew better, however, and put Jerry in at third base, as usual, like he had done all season in games in which we faced right handed pitching. Jerry knocked in 2 runs and won the game for us! That's why Ralph was the manager. And a great one at that!

Preceding Jerry in the third base spot as the "regular third baseman" was Clete Boyer, the Yankees last, "regular third baseman", one of the best fielders I had ever seen. I only got to have Clete over at third for one year, 1966, before he was traded away to the Atlanta Braves for Bill Robinson. Bill was a very talented outfielder who I had seen play in a special instructional league during the off season in Florida in 1965. Only top prospects from various organizations were invited to the special instructional program that lasted about a month. In 1966, Robinson won the Minor League Player of The Year Award and looked like he was a great acquisition for the Yankees in 1967. The other player the Yankees got in the Clete Boyer trade was a 39 year old relief pitcher, Chi Chi Olivo. Chi Chi didn't even make the team in the spring and Bill Robinson never became the player everyone thought he could be until later in his career after the Yankees traded him to the Philadelphia Phillies in 1972. He did even better after the Phillies traded him to the Pirates in 1975 where he hit very well for a few more years. With the Yankees, however, he was a real flop.

Boyer had 4 brothers that played professional baseball. I knew 2 of his younger brothers, Ronnie and Len, from the minor leagues in North Carolina. Clete's older brother, Ken, the only one I hadn't met personally, was a star for the St. Louis Cardinals in the 1960's and also played third base. Cloyd Boyer, a great guy, spent five years in the big leagues as a pitcher and was the Yankee's minor league pitching coach for the 2 ½ years I was in the minors. Cloyd helped me a lot, giving me confidence out on the mound. To put it mildly, baseball ran in the Boyer family!

Before I got to the big leagues, I thought that all the players in the major leagues could run, hit, field, and throw. After I got there I found that very few could do 3 things, much less 4. Clete could field and throw with the best of them. I never knew how much I'd miss his glove until he was gone. His replacements didn't come close to filling his spot until Graig Nettles arrived in 1973. The Braves weren't as deep as the Yankees were in the early 60's and couldn't absorb Clete's .242 batting average into their lineup in the late 60's like the Yankees could earlier that decade. Clete won a Gold Glove in the National League in 1969 when he broke Ron Santo's string of 5 Gold Glove's in a row but was released by the Braves in the early part of the season in 1971 after their general manager, Paul Richards, said he was a trouble maker. In retrospect, I sure wish the Yankees would have kept Clete for all those years. It would have given the pitching staff at least one glove man in the infield during the "Horace Clarke era" and at least a slight chance of competing against the great Oriole team in 1970.

After Clete was released from the Atlanta Braves on June 2, 1971, he still had a lot of baseball left in him. He immediately signed with the Tokyo Taiyo Whales and played for 4 years there. His old buddy, Joe Pepitone, came over to Japan in 1973 and, even though they played for different teams, they shared an apartment together in Tokyo that year. Wow! Japan is still reeling from that quienella! To be a fly on that wall!

The last time I saw Clete was at the Sheraton Hotel in New York during a reception following the Old Timers Day game in July, 2006. Clete was feeling no pain at the reception and tried to pick a fight with a sports agent, Jack Berke, for no apparent reason. Clete had bad mouthed Jack up in Cooperstown, NY a few times over the previous couple of years because Jack promoted autograph sessions using other players at his friend Arties' store, A & E Sports Cards and More, that he rented next to Clete's friends place on Main Street. It was always during the annual Hall of Fame induction ceremonies each year. Clete didn't like the competition from Jack even though Jack had made him money many times over the years by getting him appearances in New York signing autographs. Clete didn't like the fact that Jack got a fee from promoters for the players that he brought to their autograph shows. I thought I was having a bad dream at the hotel during the reception that night when Clete embarrassed himself and the entire Yankee organization (not to mention Jack Berke) when he tried to draw Jack into a fight during the cocktail hour that was held for the players, their families, and their friends. Some of the players at the reception sort of laughed it off but everyone was clearly shocked, but not surprised by Clete's behavior. Clete was not a good drinker. (Is there such a thing as a "good drinker")?

Trying to make light out of what happened that night, I sent a letter to Clete, in January 2007 as if it were from the Yankees, asking him if he would like to participate in a drinking contest the night before the Old Timers Game the following July. (SEE APPENDIX II for the letter). The winner would be given $10,000 and a lifetime supply of Crown Royal Whiskey and the right to have the 2008 contest named after him. Clete died on June 4, 2007 and obviously wouldn't have been able to make it, even if the contest had been real. He allegedly was to be pitted against Don Larsen, of the 50's, and Graig Nettles, of the 70's. Clete would have represented one of the Yankee's best drinkers of the 60's in as much as Mickey Mantle had already passed away. Sam McDowell and Ryan Duran (both ex-drinkers and legends in their own right), were to be serving the drinks, making sure they were loaded to the brim with alcohol. They also were going to be the official judges! The player who could still walk at the end of the night would be declared the winner. Paramedics would have been on hand in the event of any serious falls or seizures and a police officer would also be on duty in case of any fisticuffs.

Christmas came early before the 1973 season began. The Yankees got Nettles and got rid of Kenney all in the same day, a few weeks before Santa Claus was scheduled to come. We got Jerry Moses, along with Nettles, while the Indians got Jerry Kenney, John Ellis, Charlie Spikes, and Rusty Torres. But Nettles was "the" trade! I thought that move would finally bring me to post season play! The Yankees had just gotten what they had needed for the past 6 years. A "real" third baseman!

Right after the Nettles trade, George Steinbrenner bought the Yankees. Two months after that, the news media announced that Mike Kekich and I had traded families during the previous off season. Nettles said in his book, "Balls", that our family "trade" was the beginning of the "circus" atmosphere that would be part of his entire Yankee life until a week or 2 before the 1984 season began. Graig was traded away to San Diego because Steinbrenner got wind of Graig's book that was just about to be released, knocking Steinbrenner and a couple of Graig's teammates. While Nettles was calling the Yankees a "circus", Sparky Lyle had called them a "zoo" (in his book "The Bronx Zoo"). The Yankees were both in those days. I read both books and loved them. I really like it when people tell the truth in a book. I really enjoyed the one Richard Ben Cramer wrote about Joe DiMaggio called "The Hero's Life". I knew about a lot of the stuff that Cramer had written about in the book, and more. The funny thing about it, if you can call it that, was that there were no law suits from the DiMaggio estate or from Joe's attorney's related to some of the things Cramer wrote. So many books just sugar coat stuff that you know wasn't true, especially if you had known the players for long periods of time. One of the statements Richard made about Joe in an effort to try to describe him was, "a proud, but empty shell". As much as we don't like it, sometimes our heroes turn out to be just that.

During the National Anthem on opening day at Yankee Stadium in 1973, our new owner, George Steinbrenner finally got a chance to see what players were on his team. We all lined up along the first base foul line between home plate and first base. More importantly to George was that he got a chance to see how long everyone's hair was, and who needed haircuts. He didn't know our names yet but he did jot down certain players numbers and put them on a list that was posted in the trainers room the next day for immediate attention; haircuts! My number, #19, was on the list. Houk's number, #35, wasn't. Ralph got a pass but he'd soon pay his dues by having to hear from George daily on the dugout phone telling him how to manage the team. Nettles, who I nicknamed "Noodles", escaped the list too. He had just come from Cleveland where there was a barber shop on every corner (across from a bar), but no hippies! Had Don Zimmer been there in 1973, I'm quite sure he would have avoided the list too but many players on the team were cited for action in a barber's chair before the next home stand.

With all the knocking Steinbrenner gets, I must say that he has done more for the Yankees than any single living person I know of. He was perfect for the world's most famous sports franchise. I am proud to say that I know him.

Graig's regular nickname was "Puff". He got that name before he got to New York. It came from Graig's knack of vanishing (like a 'puff' of smoke) when it came time for retribution for a prank he had pulled on his teammates in Minnesota and in Cleveland when he had played for them. When he got to New York, I was there ready to give him a few "puffs" of my own. His first spring with the Yankees in 1973, I had my new wife steam off the labels from both a hair spray can and a deodorant can and re-glue the labels on the opposite cans. I made sure they were the same brand our clubhouse man, Pete Sheehy, normally used so as to not raise any suspicion. I then replaced the regular spray cans in the clubhouse shower area with the ones I had doctored up and then waited, and watched. I always told someone when I did stuff to another player. I usually told Mel Stottlemyre because Mel was too nice of a guy to do the things I did but I wanted him to enjoy some of the little extras that life had to offer inside the clubhouse as well. Together, Mel and I watched my (our) first victim, Graig Nettles tidy up a bit. As we hoped, Noodles sprayed deodorant on his hair and hair spray under his arms. More followed. It was great. Of course, we didn't say anything because there were many more things Graig, and the other players needed to experience before their careers would be over and they would have to return to the "real world". The clubhouse belonged to me. "Noodles" would have to hold off with his stuff until I got traded in 1974 before he could be "Puff" again. (I have a funny feeling the "puff" stood for something else as well, i.e. "puff the magic dragon")?

To this day, Noodles won't use shampoo that is yellow. That came from the time I added something to a bottle of shampoo that I shouldn't have. I wish I hadn't done it, but it was too late to take it back after I did. The first guy who used it to wash his hair was the nicest man in the universe, our bullpen coach, Jim Hegan. To my knowledge, Hegan never knew what was in that bottle with the shampoo. At least it was the same color. (Hegan died in 1984 of a heart attack. He was 63 years old). Nettles heard about it and is still paranoid to this day about the color of the shampoo he uses to wash his hair with. After you read this, you will be too! I guarantee you'll at least think about it once or twice. Maybe forever, like Noodles.

Noodles has the quickest wit of anyone I have ever seen. One night after he had won a game for us in Cleveland with one of his 390 career homeruns, a little sports writer came up to Graig and asked him a question about the kind of pitch he hit out of the park. The writer had a very obvious stuttering problem. Noodle's first words out of his mouth after the question were, "That's easy for you to say" and calmly went on to answer his question as if nothing was out of the ordinary. The writer stuttered so much it was hard to understand him but Graig figured out the question anyway. I overheard the exchange between them and couldn't believe what I had just heard. Nettles didn't even break a smile! Although everyone felt like laughing, nobody wanted to embarrass the writer so we all held off. He could drop a line on anyone, at anytime. He had a very good, dry sense of humor. (Not so funny to me was that 2 of those 390 homeruns were compliments of me)!

Graig didn't have the year that he was capable of at third during his first year with the Yankees. He was adjusting to the "Big Apple" after having come from "Little Apples": Minnesota and Cleveland. He had a career high 26 errors in 1973. Once he settled in at third, we all knew that he would be a big part of what would be happening in New York with Munson, Murcer, White, etc. in the near future. The "big guys" like Hunter, Guidry, and Jackson would come a little later, but it was obvious to everyone that Nettles was the "real" third baseman the Yankees had been waiting for.

I was having a bad year in 1973 for the first time since 1967. A lot of people blamed my bad year on the marriage thing. It really wasn't, my arm was beginning to weaken. I got one cortisone shot in my left shoulder during the middle of the year, which helped a lot, but my arm was just wearing out. Before needing that shot, I had pulled a leg muscle in the beginning of the season which caused me to start to throw differently. I noticed that the toe plate (an extra piece of leather that is sewn onto a pitchers push off spike) started wearing out toward the front of the toe plate rather than by the ball of the foot (on my left spike) where it usually wore out. It was just a nature thing, the body doing its best to protect itself from further injury. The new pitching delivery caused more stress on my shoulder making it necessary for me to get the cortisone shot around the middle of the season to be able to loosen up to pitch. That shot led to another one in spring training of 1974 for the same problem. After that, I had a hundred more, mostly off the record, over the next two years in Cleveland until my rotator cuff finally blew a hole in it the size of a quarter when I was with the Texas Rangers in 1976. I "died" on June 19, 1976.

Graig would have been a lot of fun to have as a teammate over a full career. I was barely getting to know him after a little over a year when I was traded away in the spring of 1974. I would have loved to see him interact with Steinbrenner, Reggie, and the rest. I think if I had been on the Yankees with Noodles during Reggie Jackson's years there, we would have caused Reggie to have been committed to the psychiatric ward at Belleview Hospital more than once with what we would have put him through. I was rarely caught in the "act" (of pranks) and Noodles wasn't "Puff" for nothing. I can only imagine what could have been! (I guess there's still time as alumni)!

The last time I saw Noodles was at a Phil Rizzuto/Gene Michael fund raiser in New Jersey in 2008 for a school for the blind. We had a few laughs about the "good old days". Graig reminded me of the time one of our big left-handed pitchers unleashed a big turd in a swimming pool and blamed it on a little 4 year old kid etc... (The turd was half as long as the kid)! Even though I wasn't there for that one, Noodles told me that the female life guard, the kid, and the kid's mom all ended up crying over the incident. That Holiday Inn will never be the same!

The best thing about seeing Graig in 2008 was the fact that he agreed to be my "retrieval guy" for pranks I'll be pulling on some of our alumni over the next few years. He has more access than I do to many of the former players because he gets invited to many more functions than I do. He was on pennant winning teams. I never saw a post season game other than on TV. Timing!

The reason retrieval is so important is because it completes the prank. An example of that was Moose Skowron's pace maker donation letter from the Baseball Hall of Fame. (SEE APPENDIX I for the letter). It wouldn't have been half as good without knowing how Moose told the guys at the 2006 Old Timers Game how the President of the Hall of Fame had the nerve to ask him to donate his pacemaker to the Hall. (The president didn't ask him, I did, on Hall of Fame stationery). Clete Boyer's "drinking contest" letter (SEE APPENDIX II for the letter) lacked follow up (retrieval). Although I can imagine Clete reading the letter inviting him to New York for the drinking contest, I really don't know how he reacted after reading it. I know how Moose reacted because I was there to see it. That's why Graig will be an important part to the pranks that will be flowing around the country in the next few years to Yankee alumni everywhere. Imagine, a Ron Blomberg sitting on an Island somewhere in the South Seas waiting for someone to bring him his return, first class airplane ticket back to Atlanta that "they" (some resort, etc.) promised him upon his arrival along with his stipend of $5,000 for the week. Call it "Fantasy Island". Not bad for a trip to somewhere in the South Pacific to do an autograph session for some Israeli separatist group of some kind or another. Or, how about a little known, ex-player like Ross Moschito flying down to Disney World to judge a beauty pageant for the Southeast United States Region, looking for the contact person at the front gate of Disney World who was supposed to meet him there dressed in a Yankee uniform. The "contact person" (who never was) that Ross thought would be giving him his fee of $2,000 in cash and a first class return air ticket back to New York after the weekend for judging the pageant; a weekend that 'never was', at least in anyone's mind but Ross's—and mine. We'll call that one, "When You Wish Upon a Star". (Hint for Yankee alumni: don't go anywhere without a round trip airplane ticket in your hand before you leave home).

Graig would have appreciated what I really wanted to do when I found out that my arm surgery didn't help prolong my career and I would be out of baseball. I was in Sarasota, Florida in 1977 with the Chicago White Sox and my "man", Bill Veeck, trying to make his team after rotator cuff surgery the October before. The chances of me pitching again were slim but I was not ready to leave baseball without giving it my best shot. After my arm "fell off" on the mound that spring, (it felt like it anyway), I had to ask the manager of the White Sox, Bob Lemon to mercifully take me out of my first, only, and last spring training game for the Chicago White Sox or for anyone. (Lemon really wanted me to make the team because he knew I could drink. His dream was to own a bar on a beach in Hawaii when he retired and be its only customer. I'd have fit in with him very well). My arm just wouldn't work after facing my only batter for the St. Louis Cardinals. I couldn't even get the ball to home plate on the fly! It was a lonely feeling knowing I was finally "dead", a term I had coined (I died, he died, etc.) for either sustaining a serious injury, going through a trade, or being released by a team. My first thought when I was coming out of the game was, "where do dead people go after they die"? They end up in a casket.

I really wanted to rent a casket for a day and have the local funeral home bring it over to Payne Park, in Sarasota and set it up in the stands so I could sign my final autographs, as a ball player, from a casket at the park where I had thrown my last pitch. How fitting. Bill Veeck always sat in the stands and signed autographs with his wooden leg showing! Why shouldn't I leave baseball in a casket signing my final autographs? Veeck would have loved it. After all, he was the king of promotions. I wanted so bad to do it but didn't because of the huge amount of publicity I had gotten in 1973 because of our marital situation. That would have stirred the whole situation up again. I didn't care, personally, but I knew my wife would have hated it. The players would have loved it as much as Veeck, especially Noodles! I wish I had done it! My wife would have forgiven me, eventually. Maybe I'll do a "book signing" in a casket somewhere?

Eternally speaking, I'm quite sure Clete will be doing "time" in the "lake". How long, only God knows. What I do know is that it won't be for his drinking. Drinking doesn't preclude a person from Heaven, even if the person is a drunk. (Noah tied one on from time to time!) Unbelief does! From what I know about Clete's faith, I don't think he was a believer when he died in 2007. If that was the case, there's a very good chance that he will be the starting third baseman for the same team that Billy Martin will be on, the team that will be wearing the red uniforms and the asbestos underwear. His graduation date will depend on how well his rehab program goes. His brother Cloyd will be on the other team, the one dressed in the white uniforms. I don't know what team Clete's other brothers will be on. God knows.

Jerry Kenney is a very nice, humble guy. He had a strong biblical upbringing from his family and I've heard that he is a believer. I'm not certain. Nobody but God is. But I would guess that Jerry is a "first round draft choice". He won't be in the starting lineup for the All Saints team, but he will be on the "2 billion man roster".

The starting third baseman on the team dressed in white might be Graig Nettles. Right now, he is on the "disabled list" but could become activated pretty soon. He had prostate cancer surgery in 2008 which tends to get a person's attention and might just help him become an active "first round draft choice" before his 'release' (death). I sure hope so. I want to hear more Reggie Jackson stories without having to wait hundreds or thousands of years!

CHAPTER **14**

Even Met Fans Go To Heaven!

I grew up in the Chicagoland area where my dad was a very solid Chicago White Sox fan. I emulated him and became a Sox fan too. I lived and breathed the White Sox during my youth where my heroes were #2, Nelson Fox and #19, Billy Pierce. Little Nellie was a second baseman and Pierce was a hard throwing left-handed pitcher. Being a White Sox fan in Chicago, I couldn't possibly be a Cub fan as well. It just wasn't done in Chicago and was even more complicated in New York where fans had 3 teams to choose from before 1958. Because of it, I quite naturally "hated" the Cubs and thought of them, and the whole National League, as the "minor leagues". The White Sox, and the American League, were the "big leagues" to me. All the games, when I was a kid, were televised on Channel 9 (WGN) in Chicago. When I turned on our TV, if I saw Wrigley Field in the background, I instantly thought, "minor league". In contrast, when I saw the White Sox background (Comiskey Park), I thought, "real thing". That "belief", or "feeling", followed me to New York when I became a big leaguer in 1966 with the American League's New York Yankees. I came to New York naturally hating the Mets, and still do, despite having some good friends that are ex-

Mets. Ron Swoboda is one of them. I still can't believe the catch he made in the World Series in 1969!

I can't imagine anyone from New York (or anywhere for that matter) being a Met fan, especially with the Yankees residing in the same town! I can understand how someone from New York could have been a Brooklyn Dodger or New York Giant fan when the teams were still in New York. But a Met fan, not! I can even see someone in New York liking the Phillies or the Pittsburg Pirates if they preferred the National over the American League, but a Met fan—I don't think so. The Met's are nothing and came from nowhere! At least the Phillies and Pirates have some "legitimate" history.

The Mets played their first season in the Polo Grounds across the Harlem River from historic Yankee Stadium in 1962 while their first home, Shea Stadium, was being built in the Queens to begin playing in it for the first time in 1964. Citi Field then took over as the Met's new home in April, 2009. The Mets were created to appease Brooklyn Dodger and New York Giant fans who had been abandoned by their teams when both opted for better markets and better weather just before the 1958 season began. National League fans in New York were left with nothing for 4 years until the Mets surfaced in 1962 out of nowhere, 59 years after the Yankees franchise first began in New York back in 1903.

The Mets owners also had hoped to attract the many Yankee "haters" in New York. Most of those "haters" were comprised of immature baseball fans who were envious of the Yankee's dominance and successes beginning with the days they first occupied their historic "House That Ruth Built" in 1923. The number of championships the Yankees racked up in the 20th century (25 of them, and another in the year 2000) remains unprecedented with any professional sports franchise. The Met's, in comparison, have only been World Champs twice in their short, insignificant team history.

The only excuse I could possibly imagine for a person becoming a Met fan would be that his or her parents happened to have liked the Mets for some reason and they were just following in their parents footsteps. Once they became adults and learned something about baseball, their excuse for remaining a Met fan should have dissipated.

When I got to New York in 1966, I was really proud being a Yankee, especially with all the history associated with the franchise. We had all the big names (except for Tony Kubek) that had been on pennant winners from 1960-1964 during which time the Mets were just starting off with their new franchise. The Met's had hired an icon from the Yankee's past, Casey Stengel, in an effort to gain some instant credibility in New York market. They rented a piece of Yankee history to manage the team for their first 4 years (1962-1965). Except for the 1961 season, Casey had managed the Yankees for 12 straight years (1949-1960) prior to taking the Mets job.

When I first got to New York, I couldn't understand how anyone could go to a Met game and see "nobodies" when they could come across town to the Bronx and see the "real thing". The Yankees still had "real" players like Mantle, Maris, Howard, Richardson, Bouton, Ford, Stottlemyre, Pepitone, Tresh, etc. etc… The Mets had nothing but a broken down, retired, old ex-Yankee manager, a bunch of "has been" ballplayers, and a few kids.

I was astounded when the Yankees finished in last place in the American League in 1966, something they hadn't done since 1912! The Mets came in second to last in the National League in 1966, but we were New York's cellar dwellers! The Mets would go to the bottom of the barrel again in 1967 while the Yankees moved up a notch to 9th place but sadly enough, in 1967, that year our team was actually worse than the 1966 Yankee group. The Yankees were struggling while the Mets were beginning to reap the talents of some of their young pitching investments like Tom Seaver and Jerry Koosman. It wasn't a happy time for Yankee fans but at least we still had #7, Mickey Mantle, #9, Roger Maris, and #16, Whitey Ford in Yankee uniforms! The Met's really didn't even need numbers on the backs of their player's uniforms during their first few years! Nobody, including their own manager, Casey Stengel, knew their names anyway!

Tom Seaver was really a great pitcher, obviously, but was a nice guy too. I remember crossing paths with him in LaGuardia Airport one night when the Mets were returning from a road trip at the same time we were leaving New York on a road trip of our own. Seaver happened to have watched our game on TV the day before and when he saw me at the airport he offered me a suggestion about staying "on top" on my curveball a little bit more. (I was dropping my arm down on my curveball, making it flat and easier to hit). He realized that I had struggled somewhat for the entire game with all my breaking stuff. I thought that was really nice of him to do despite the fact that I had already nicknamed him "Nancy" (his wife's first name). I had sensed that he was a little henpecked, like I was at the time. They did appear to be the perfect couple, however, especially living in the New York area full time. Maybe I was jealous?

I always felt a little sad for Seaver to have been traded a couple of times before he retired. It would have been so much better for him, and the Met's, to have kept him a "one team player" like Mantle, Ford, and Stottlemyre had been with the Yankees. He never looked right in a Cincinnati Red's or Chicago White Sox uniform much less ending his career in Boston Red Sox attire! What a sad way to finish such a sterling career. Babe Ruth went out of baseball in a Red Sox uniform the same way 51 years before "Tom Terrific" (Seaver); as did Elston Howard in 1968. At least Ruth and Howard didn't have to wear a Met's uniform on their journeys. I wish I could say the same thing about my buddy, Stottlemyre, who succumbed in the 80's and coached for the Mets for a few years (1984-1993). At least Mel never threw a pitch as a NY Met!

Despite my distain for the Mets, eternal things are much more important than team rivalry. The fact is, God is good and will really prove it when He takes even Met fans with Him to Heaven when it's all over and done with. God is no respecter of man (or woman), nor of what team someone favors. If He were, Heaven's "sky boxes" would be reserved only for Yankee fans while the bleachers would be full of Met fans with their crooked little, orange "NY's" on their medium blue baseball caps. I envision this during the 1,000 year millennial game (played in the new Yankee Stadium) after the Lord has returned to earth. Met fans will all be dressed in bright red clothing whereas the Yankee fans will be decked out in lily white garments. (That is the period of time in which all Israel will be saved, whether they were Met fans or not). When the game ends, however, the banquet will begin and will include everyone who ever lived. Yankees and their fans will be brothers and sisters with their previous cross town Met rivals and everyone will be part of one big, very happy family, a situation that before would have been impossible. (Isaiah 11:6-10, wolves = Met's fans, and lambs = Yankee fans, will dwell together peacefully).

If you remember when our country united for a short time after the 9/11 attacks in 2001, when God finally becomes All in All, the end of the ages will be fantastic! Everyone will be on a winner and all tears will be wiped away. Hell will itself be cast into the "lake of fire" and everyone in it will graduate and spend eternity in Heaven eating hot dogs with Babe Ruth and Ron Swoboda!

There is one "slight" problem. Many players and fans, along with multitudes of the general population will be spending time in the "lake of fire" before they get "moved up" ("graduate") to Heaven. The reason will be because they didn't trust Christ as their personal Lord and Saviour while they were still alive on the earth. While their "dip" or "swim" in the "lake of fire" will not last forever, as most have been taught to believe, the rehab program will be very unpleasant. The time spent in "the lake" (of fire) will not be for torture, like most think, but for purification and refining. It will involve whatever training will be necessary to help reconcile a person back to the Lord, His ultimate purpose for mankind. As former preacher and theologian, John Wesley put it, "Punishment will last no longer than is necessary to bring man to hate his sin and be reconciled to his Saviour".

Thank goodness that there's still time for people to avoid the "dip" and become "first round draft choices" like Mantle, Murcer, Richardson, and millions of others. The way is simple but must be sincere. It involves accepting the Lord as their personal Lord and Saviour.

I pray that my friend, Thurman Munson did so before he died after his plane crashed on August 2, 1979. If he didn't, I'll never know. Regardless, I will still see him again at the end of the ages, and that will be forever! I have the same prayer, and hope, for you too!

CHAPTER **15**

Everything's Going to Be OK!

(When my friend, contemporary Christian writer, Phil Yancey, found out the name of my book, he e-mailed me and said, "If Mickey's in heaven, that should help the rest of us", 10/27/07). That's the point!

If Paul Harvey had any problems, they vanished on February 28th, 2009. Paul Harvey was a "first round draft choice"! He was surrounded by his family when he passed away at the age of 90.

During a road trip to Baltimore in 1972, my wife Marilyn, Mike, and his wife and I joked about our situation being on Paul Harvey's program, "The rest of the story" some day. That day came; we 'were' his show for a day in 1973! Mr. Harvey ended the segment saying, "The two players say it won't affect their play on the field". It did. Mike was traded.

Famous radio and TV psychologist, Dr. Joyce Brothers commented about our situation in 1973 saying that only one of "the couples" would "make it" (stay together). She was right. Mike's wife and I made it, Mike and my wife Marilyn didn't. Dr. Brothers almost didn't "make it" herself in 1959 after the media thought that she cheated when she won the grand prize on "The $64,000 Question" quiz show. (In those days, the media figured that a "woman" could never know that much about boxing, the topic she and the show's sponsor had agreed on). Even though she eventually proved that she was "innocent", the public still remembers the "association" to this day.

The public will never remember that I pitched to Willie McCovey in the 1970 All Star Game and won 20 games on the final day of that season, but they sure won't forget my marriages! A few years from now, ask Pete Rose, Mark McGwire, Barry Bonds, Roger Clemens, and Alex Rodriguez what the public remembers. Who said elephants have the best memories!

Ask any of "Shoeless Joe Jackson's" descendants, if he has any, what people think of when "Shoeless Joe's" name is mentioned even 90 years after the "Black Sox scandal" in 1919.

When we get to age 65+ and our children are all (almost) raised and our bodies begin to go on the "disabled list", there's more than the nursing home to look forward to. There are memories.

I was invited to a baseball card show in February, 2009 across from LaGuardia Airport in Queens, NY, to sign a few hundred autographs. While I was in New York, I went to visit our faithful old Yankee photographer, Luis Requena, who lives in a small apartment in midtown Manhattan. While I was with him in the apartment, I saw the excitement he showed for everything that he had experienced with the Yankees during his 50+ years behind the lens. Luis was one of the great photographers in New York that helped capture parts of Yankee history on his old fashioned box camera (before the digital age). He got more than photos out of his career. He got memories. I could see them in his eyes! Even unshaven and in his pajamas at 3:00 in the afternoon, the 89 year old said he had "lived a life with no regrets". I may not ever see Luis again on this earth, and won't see my dear friend, the late Fr. Joe Dispenza, but I will never forget the glow in both of their eyes concerning the time they spent with, and around, the Yankees during their lifetimes.

I am now the oldest person in my family and although I'd rather not be the next one to die, if I am, I can truly say that I've lived a life that few have had the privilege to live, in pinstripes. Those Yankee years top the list of wonderful experiences and memories I've ever had.

I can't even believe I was ever on the field in the original "house that Ruth built", much less having been the starting pitcher for the last game ever played there! It's hard to imagine that I was actually out there, between the very same foul lines where the "Babe" himself actually pitched and pounded out so many home runs! It is even more unbelievable to think that I ended up having the best ERA of ALL TIME in Yankee Stadium! A "nobody" (me) from a little town in Illinois who's dad was the one who started Little League there (Mt. Prospect, IL) in 1950, ending up being #1 in a category that will stand up for "all time" at historic Yankee Stadium in New York? No way!

It would have been nice to have been in a World Series or even just a post season game in Yankee Stadium but during my time frame in baseball with the Yankees, 1966-1974, it wasn't going to be. In retrospect, however, I would have rather been a New York Yankee on a losing team than a New York Met or an Oakland Athletic on a World Series winner! No kidding!

When I was a rookie in 1966 I stayed at the Manhattan Hotel in the city for a couple of months at the beginning of the season. I rode the subway, and loved it. It was a great experience and it saved me time and money. Once in a while, someone would even recognize me and say, "Nice game yesterday", or something like that. I'm sure that I zoomed past Mickey Mantle a few times on the subway I was riding in while he was "up top" in his cab from the St. Moritz Hotel on 59th Street through Central Park on his way to Yankee Stadium. (He could afford it, I couldn't).

While I was at the card show in February, 2009, I elected to take the subway again, for old time's sake, 43 years later. I could have jumped in a cab offered to me by the owner of Foley's NY, Shaun Clancy, but I wanted to see if riding on the subway still felt the same as it did in 1966. I had been invited to Foley's, the great Irish Pub on 33rd Street, for an autograph signing gig that the agent I use for private signings, Joe Quagliano, set up for me while I was in

New York. While I was at Foley's, I stumbled in on a radio show that the pub was hosting with Mark Healey and Joe Janish of Baseball Digest. I went on their live show not knowing Joe was such a huge Met fan. I think I made an ass of myself for bashing the Met's (like I always do), but Joe was not offended. I did mean what I said however. We all sat down and laughed about it after the show was over. Good guys. It was fun being "somebody" again, even for just a couple of days.

The subways (trains, or whatever the New Yorkers call them) were older than I had remembered and the people riding on them didn't look real happy. Eye contact was still an absolute "no no". It was fun for me and did, indeed, bring back fond memories of the good old days. I had purchased an "all day pass" (Metrocard) for $7.50 and could ride anywhere I wanted to for the whole day. I was in hog heaven! On my February, 2009, subway ride, nobody recognized me. (That was a good thing; I'm in hiding because of this book and a movie they're making about us. I want to stay out of the public eye for my family's sake. We are enjoying anonymity nowadays traveling around the country from New York to Colorado).

After I left Luis Requena's apartment on 23rd Street, I took a bus to 59th Street to have dinner at Mickey Mantle's Restaurant with Marty Appel.

Marty had been the person who first told me that I had made the All Star team in 1970. At the time, Marty was the assistant Public Relations man for the Yankees under the Yankee Public Relations legend, Bob Fischel. Looking at all of the pictures of Mantle brought back memories of another time. It seemed just like yesterday in a way, but in another way it had been so long ago that it felt like I hadn't even been there. Marty helped bring me back in time to re-live some of my Yankee moments, good ones and bad ones alike.

One of those bad ones came when I was pitching in the last game in the "house that Ruth built" on September 30, 1973. We had a 4-2 lead in the top of the 8th inning when I gave up 2 singles in a row. Houk almost always took his starting pitchers out of the game from the 6th inning on if they were ahead in the score and if they allowed the tying run to get on base. That way, the starter couldn't get a loss, but still could be the winner. At worst, he could get a "no decision". When Ralph came out to make the pitching change, it allowed the 30,000+ fans in attendance that day to vent all their frustrations out on him for the Yankees failures over the past 9 seasons. (Ralph got to experience a little of the same feeling I had in spring training that year when I got a standing room only booing from the fans in St. Petersburg, FL. That was the day I made my first public appearance on the mound since our "deal" had hit the papers). If I could have finished the last 2 innings, the fans would never have gotten to single out, and boo Ralph. It was like thousands of people booing my own dad for something he didn't do, right in front of me! I got a "no decision" for the day and that night, Ralph Houk gave up his Yankee uniform and resigned!

It would be 2 years before the Yankees would return to their refurbished home (1976) which they would finally move out of after the 2008 season. The "new" Yankee Stadium was ready for them in April, 2009 just a block away from the "original one". All records for the new stadium began on opening day, 2009. To me, however, the "House That Ruth Built" was the only "real" Yankee Stadium. When we said goodbye to Yankee Stadium after the game on September 30, 1973, part of Babe Ruth, Joe DiMaggio, Mickey Mantle, Whitey Ford and the rest of the Yankees went with it.

For me, 1973 started with a boo and ended with a boo, even though the last "boo" wasn't specifically for me. The last boo was for what became known as the "Horace Clark era" of Yankee history by baseball historians.

After having posted a losing season in 1973, and the Yankees having been sentenced to a 2 year "prison term" in Shea Stadium, baseball wasn't fun anymore. Being traded to Cleveland was almost a relief at that point!

Facing my buddies, Munson & Murcer, for the first time as opposing hitters was really odd. Seeing their faces looking out at me was almost funny. I remember both of them smiling out at me when they got into the batters box, almost like they were saying, "I don't want to get a hit off you but I've got to make it look good. I really hope you beat us". These 2 guys were like the "Yankees of old", the ones who would run down their own grandmother at home plate to win a game for the Yankees! The feelings I had were multifold! In a way, it was like old home week, but at the same time it felt very lonely not being on "their team" anymore. (I can't believe they're both dead)!

By that time, the "meaning of baseball" was gone for me. It then became just a means of earning a living. First it was with the Cleveland Indians, then the Texas Rangers, each time getting further away from where I had been "somebody" on the Yankees, the only place that ever felt like home. Even though I was with my new, wonderful wife, and her precious little daughters, I had lost my "team" and worse yet, my sons. The end of my career would come next.

At the end of the line with the Texas Rangers in 1976, I "found the Lord". If it hadn't been for that, and my new wife, I don't know what would have happened. The Lord really "saved" me, literally and figuratively. Other than that, I was busted.

It really wasn't until I was invited to the Yankee Fantasy Camp in 2004 that I felt like a "somebody" again. Even though I was a "little overweight" and couldn't throw anymore, putting on a Yankee uniform made me feel alive again. I realized the magic of what being a Yankee really meant. Many thanks to the directors of the Yankee Fantasy Camp, Patrick Scanlon and Julie Kremer, for giving me my Yankee uniform back. (Thanks to Debbie Nicolosi and Michael Bonner as well for their parts in "keeping me a Yankee")! If I were to "vanish" (die) today, like my buddy Johnny Blanchard did on March 25, 2009, I will have finished up being a very "happy camper"! (I had mixed feelings at Blanchard's funeral on March 30, 2009. The note in the handout at his wake said, "He left us quietly, his thoughts unknown, but left us a memory, we are proud to own; so treasure him Lord, in your garden of rest, for when on earth, he was one of the best." That he was! Like his handout said "his thoughts unknown". That was the part that bothered me for Johnny's sake. I wasn't sure what his relationship with the Lord was when he died. We never talked about it. I guess nobody really knows but the person himself and God! I do know that Johnny is at rest. I'm sure glad I knew him and know that I'll see him again someday).

At one of those Yankee Fantasy Camps in January, 2007, I actually broke down and cried at the Saturday night banquet that week after seeing a picture of Mel Stottlemyre and me with our arms around each other on top of the dugout steps. (I am not a crier. I didn't cry at either my mom or dad's funerals or even at Munson's for that matter)! The picture brought back many memories I had with Mel over the years, along with the thoughts of all that he and his family went through with the death of their 11 year old son, Jason, to Leukemia in 1981 and then Mel's own battle with multiple myeloma in 1999, which, thank the good Lord, he is winning. The realization that my new wife and I had not been around Mel and his wonderful wife, Jean, over the past 33 years, and what we had been through ourselves over the years (including my own cancer), was just too much. I couldn't help sobbing like a baby. It went "deep". I really love Mel and Jean and realized it at that moment. It was overwhelming.

When Thurman Munson died in 1979, I never knew how close I had been to him. On my 3 day trip to New York in February, 2009, I stopped over to the Grand Hyatt Hotel NY on 42nd Street and dropped off a note for Thurman's wife, Diane. They were having the 29th Annual Thurman Munson Awards Dinner that night. I at least wanted to let Diane know that we were still thinking about her and about all the great times we had together. I told Diane in the note how much I missed "Tug boat" (one of my nicknames for Thurman), and how much I had appreciated how she, Kay Murcer, and Jean Stottlemyre had accepted the "new us". They made my new wife feel so at home with them after our famous family "trade" had been made public in 1973. They were great to both of us! The players were too!

I wish I could go back in time and have the talk with Thurman now that I was going to have with him 2 days before he died in 1979. I was going to talk to him about where he might spend eternity when he died. In 1979 I would have told him that unless he became "born again", (which he didn't believe in), that if he were to die, he would spend eternity in hell. I would have sounded like the Pastor of Moody Church, Erwin Lutzer, in his book, "One Minute After You Die", a preview of a person's 'final' destination. Lutzer's book outlined either "eternal hell" for an unbeliever or "eternal life" for a believer. It is the same thing that almost all of the mainline preachers would tell you today. (It's no wonder why so many church goers are so confused. It's hard to intertwine a "loving God", who says He will never leave us or forsake us on the one hand, (Bobby Murcer's favorite verse—Deuteronomy 31: 6), and dangling an "eternal hell" out there in His other hand in the event that He decides to go back on His word and finally give up on us, forever! That type of illogical doctrine would be perplexing to anyone)!

I would not tell him the same thing today, after 3+ years studying about God's grace that I would have told him in 1979. I would tell Thurman today that it was OK if he didn't believe in the "born again thing". Thurman was a Catholic. Catholic's, in general, don't believe the "born again thing" like Evangelicals do. In a way, it's just a matter of semantics. (In this, I believe the Catholics are 'right on' by looking at salvation on a daily basis). I would also tell him that it would be great if he did trust the Lord as his personal Lord and Saviour (& maybe he did), but even if he didn't, he would not spend eternity in hell, no matter what he did, or didn't do. Nobody will!

Erwin Lutzer, Charles Stanley, St. Augustine, and the rest of the ones who preach that are wrong! (Having to go to hell is one thing, but going to hell FOREVER is quite another story, and an incorrect one at that). I would make sure to tell him that if he stayed close to the "real" Bible that his life would have way more meaning and he would have much more peace than if he didn't. I surely wouldn't hang the "eternal hell" thing over his head in fear, like many Churches and denominations do today, and have done since the 5th Century A.D. Instead, I would focus on the love of God that will never leave us or forsake us. I would tell him that God will be there "as long as it takes" for him to come "home" where we all belong.

I am convinced that if I would have had enough time with Thurman that he would know that it wouldn't have mattered whether he was a Catholic, a Lutheran, a Jew, a Muslim or even a New York Met. God would be there to welcome him whenever he was ready, regardless of the label he wore. I would tell him that even though he wasn't raised within the conventional church like many of us were, that "church people" have the hardest time of any group understanding the conclusions I have come to. They believe just about everything they hear from their pulpits, just as most readers believe anything they see in print just because it's in print. On top of that, almost everybody's parents believe(d) in an everlasting hell for the "unsaved". The reason their parents believed it was because they too had been taught the "concept" by well meaning clergy and their own parents. The chain keeps going on and on right down the line. I'd finish up telling him that most "church people" have one final stumbling block, their own Bible! Most "translations" use terms like "eternal damnation" or "everlasting torment", etc. referring to hell, confusing 99% of the readers. In the original languages, (Greek & Hebrew) the "real" Bible doesn't say, or mean that at all!

I believe that once Thurman "crossed over the bridge" (of faith) that he wouldn't have cared what people thought about what he said. He'd just say it. That's the way he was. (Check out the glossary at the end of this book to see why I believe what I believe and why I think Thurman would have understood the same thing too).

In searching for the answer about my own salvation I found that "if grace is true", (and it is), it is true for everyone. It's not just for people like Billy Graham, Mickey Mantle, Mother Teresa and me. It's for everyone! All means all! The price was already paid for all of us 2,000+ years ago. When we realize it, (get "converted", or whatever you want to call it), our lives will be different. Life is tough at times but God is good all the time! Thurman knew my friend Fr. Joe Dispenza quite well and would have appreciated what Fr. Joe said when a few of us put him on the spot and asked him the tough question, "What 'group', religiously speaking, was right when it came to salvation, and who goes to Heaven?" Fr. Joe's answer summed it all up when he said, "See you at the end"! Fr. Joe knew. I know now too! It's been a long road trip, but eventually the final game will be over and--everything's going to be OK!

Relax, love, and trust God.

Final box score: Yankees 1,000,000,000,000 , Mets ----- "to be determined at the end of the ages"! Number of people in attendance: Everyone!

Like Fr. Joe said, "See you at the end"!

Fritz Peterson, #19.

PS. Bernie Madoff is a New York Met fan!

Appendix I

National Baseball Hall of Fame and Museum, Inc.
25 Main Street
Cooperstown, New York 13326-0590
1-888-HALL-OF-FAME
607-547-2044 FAX

Bill "Moose" Skowron
c/o Chicago White Sox,
35 & Shields Ave.
Chicago, IL 60616

Dear Mr. Skowron,

Hope this letter finds you in good health and in good spirits.

Our staff has found out from the Chicago Tribune that you have a pacemaker. Thank goodness for modern medicine!

The reason that I am writing is to ask whether you would be interested in donating it (when you pass of course) to the Hall of Fame to either auction off, or to place by your good friend Mickey Mantles' display at the Hall of Fame in his honor?

Talk it over with your family and please get back to me as soon as possible. Call me collect if you would like at 607-547-7200.

Continued success with the Chicago White Sox!

My Best Wishes,

Dale A. Petroskey, President

Appendix II

New York Yankees

TICKET OFFICE
YANKEE STADIUM
BRONX, NEW YORK 10451
(212) 293-6000

EXECUTIVE OFFICE
YANKEE STADIUM
BRONX, NEW YORK 10451
(212) 293-4300

Dear Mr. Boyer.   1/04/07

We are scheduling a special event for the day before Old Timers Day, 2007 and would like to invite you and a guest to attend. It will be called the 1st Annual "Get All The Gusto in Life Talent Show" featuring a drinking contest between you. Don Larsen, and Graig Nettles.

Mr. Larsen (who has already committed to attend and participate) will be representing the 1956 pennant winning Yankees. You would represent the last place 1966 Yankees, and Mr. Nettles would represent the pennant winning 1976 Yankee club if he accepts the invitation.

The judges for the contest will be former Yankees Sam McDowell and Ryne Duren, both hard throwers and pretty good drinkers in their day. Their decision will be final.

The winner will receive a check for $10,000 and will have the right to have the contest named after him for the following year as well as getting a lifetime supply of Crown Royal Whiskey, Canada's finest blend since 1939 (not to exceed a fifth a day).

ESPN has agreed to film the entire event and of course will be very sensitive in its presentation as to protect the image of our National Pastime, i.e., baseball, Chevrolet and apple pie.

All your expenses will be paid for and 2 tickets will be given to you for the Old Timers game on Saturday should you decide to attend. The winner will be announced before the Old Timers Day Game Saturday afternoon. Transportation to and from the airport, hotel and ballpark will be provided as usual. The "contest" will occur on Friday night so game tickets that night will not be necessary.

We sure hope you will join us and please call collect ASAP so we can make arrangements for you early or find a replacement to represent the 60's.

Sincerely,

Tony Moranti, Special Events Coordinator
718-293-4300

187

Appendix III

Global Missions Statistics--2000

Number of followers:

1,100,000,000	— Muslims
1,000,000,000	— Roman Catholics
890,000,000	— Hindus
875,000,000	— Non-religious/atheists
680,000,000	— Evangelicals (11% of the worlds population)
340,000,000	— Buddhists
340,000,000	— Chinese Folk Religions
220,000,000	— Tribal Religious
17,000,000	— Judaism
5,486,200,000	— estimated worlds population in the year 2,000

A.W Tozer and Billy Graham have stated that only 10-15% of the Evangelical Church members are actually "saved" ("born again"). Tozer and Graham do not consider Catholics or "Protestant non-evangelicals" as being "saved".

Assuming that Tozer and Graham are correct, about 12½% of the 680,000,000 Evangelicals-- or 85,000,000 people (2%) who were living in the world in the year 2,000 will be going to heaven, forever!

The remaining 5,401,200,000 people (98%) who were living in the world in the year 2,000 will be going to hell, forever!

Keith Morrison, of NBC News wrote in an article in August, 2006, "Hell is for other people!" that "75% of Americans felt pretty sure they will be going to heaven when they died while only 2% expected they would wind up in hell".

Which way is it? 2% going to Heaven, or 2% going to hell?

Another Survey by Baylor University in 2008 stated that Americans think that 50% of them will be going to Heaven and 50% will be going to hell, forever!

What percentage of the people will be going to Heaven? Think about it.

2%   Like the Global Missions Statistics 2,000 indicate?
50%   Like Baylor University's 2008 Survey suggests?
75%   In a survey sited by Keith Morrison in 2006 (of Americans only)?
100% Stated in the Bible 2,000+ years ago when God finally becomes All in All.

Glossary of Terms

This book is not intended to be a theological study. I have said a few things in this book that many church-goers might question so I wanted to explain some of these items by defining a few basic terms found in the Bible and in this book. I believe the Bible is God's Word, but I also believe there are very few believers who really understand the Bible due to the fact that it has been distorted by church traditions as well as the opinions of men. Most people that attend a church assume their pastor is teaching the correct things concerning the Bible as it was intended, by God, to be understood. In actuality, they are wrong on some major points. Before any might suggest that the majority of preachers, teachers and scholars within the church cannot be wrong, let me remind you that spiritual truth was never understood by the majority. The prophets of old were in the minority, as was Jesus in His day. The church that was addressed by the apostles Peter and Paul had rejected both of them before the end of their lifetimes. (See 2 Timothy 1:15; 4:16). What makes us think the majority within the church finally got everything figured out? No! If we want to understand spiritual truth and correct Bible teachings we cannot expect to find it within the "traditional church" of our day. We must seek to study the Bible for ourselves, casting off the biases from any particular organized church, preacher, Bible teacher or scholar, and think for ourselves.

AION (OR EON)

One of the most misunderstood words in the Bible. The Greek word "aion" and its Hebrew equivalent "olam" clearly do not mean endless or eternal, but refer to fixed periods of time with a beginning and an end. Thus the many variations we see in the Scriptures ... eon (singular), eons (plural), before the eons, at the end of the eons, the eon of the eons, etc. Most Bible translations treat this word very inconsistently, sometimes using "eternal" and other times "age" when eternal will not fit the context. But such inconsistent handling of the word causes much of what God has revealed to us to be lost or confused.

AIONIAN (OR EONIAN)

Something that takes place during one eon, or during several eons.

ALL IN ALL

It is God's plan to become All in all. All will be subjected to God, and reconciled to God. We observe that currently God may be All in some, but He is not yet All in all.

Christ is "the One completing the all in all" (Ephesians 1:23). It is through Christ that all are being reconciled to God (Colossians 1:20). The body of Christ is the complement of Christ (Ephesians 4:14); "the complement of the One completing the all in all" (Ephesians 1:23). Our "Great Commission" is found in 2 Corinthians 5:18-21. We are to proclaim the message of reconciliation to God.

We see God finally becoming All in all in 1 Corinthians 15:28; once

Christ has accomplished His mission to bring all into subjection. We see in 1 Corinthians 15:22-28 that there is no longer any need for sovereignties or authorities, and the final enemy (death) is abolished as God becomes All in all.

If the lake of fire was still burning, all would not yet be reconciled to God, and God would not yet be All in all. In this world we see chaos and tribulations all around us, but things will not always be in this state. God is in the process of becoming All in all.

AUGUSTINE
See St. Augustine.

"BELIEVER"
A "believer" is one who believes God. We read that Abraham believed God, and it was reckoned to him as righteousness. We are not given an exhaustive list of exactly what Abraham believed, and some of his decisions seemed to display a degree of doubt or misunderstanding as to what God had in mind (e.g. fathering a son through Hagar, instead of waiting on God to deliver Isaac through Sarah). But whatever the specifics, we simply read that Abraham believed God and it was reckoned as righteousness.

Churches today like to create lists of what one must believe to be a Christian. These lists vary from one church to another, so that should tell us something. Some say we must believe in the concept of the Trinity. Others say we must believe that hell is eternal. Some say we must be water baptized. Some even specify the precise mode of water baptism.

The problem is that we are often driven by the fear of what God will do to us if we don't believe all of the right things. One slip and we think that makes us a non-believer and destined for eternal torment.

We are thinking in terms of what we must believe, at a minimum, to be "saved." We place no real trust in God and His grace. We think we must **do** something to be saved, even if this **doing** is simply mustering-up the right formula of belief.

But there is not really a formula or list of what one must believe. The fact is that through God's Word, and through the person of His Son, God has spoken. We are asked to believe. Period. We don't fully understand all details, and some understand more details than others, but we are not asked to fully understand all details of God's revelation; but only to believe.

Here's something else to think about. If believing was something we could muster-up on our own, we could boast about that, couldn't we? I could say I am smarter than those who don't believe, since I have the intelligence to believe while they do not. But aren't we told that salvation is totally a gift from God, lest any should boast? (Ephesians 2:9)

I don't think anyone could be a believer, unless God enables that person to believe. Without God's help, the entire world would be non-believers destined for God's judgment. But rather than abandon this hopeless lot called humanity, God chooses **SOME** and enables them to believe, not because He loves them more, but because He has a purpose for them that will lead to **ALL** being reconciled to God. That's God's method; to choose **SOME** to act as His instruments so that **ALL** will ultimately be reconciled to Him.

If you think that every person has the ability, on his own, to become a believer by having enough intelligence to believe, consider the following verses:

The apprehensions of the unbelievers are blinded by the god of this eon (Satan).2 Cor 4:3

To the Philippians belief on Christ was "graciously granted." Philippians 1:29

Not one is just; not one is understanding; and not one is seeking out God. Romans 3:10-11

With all of this being true, is it even possible for a single person to believe on their own? Or, like Lydia (Acts 16:14), are we dependent upon God to open up our heart to believe?

DANTE'S INFERNO

A poetic work by a secular philosopher, Dante Alighieri, written in 1472. This poem has influenced the concept of hell as a place of endless torment. As a matter of fact, more weight has been placed upon this work than the Bible itself, in terms of our beliefs concerning hell.

"DIP" IN THE LAKE, OR A "SWIM" IN THE LAKE ("OF FIRE")

The Bible does not provide a great amount of information concerning the lake of fire. Does one who experiences the lake experience a second death like the first death, where there is no consciousness? Or is the second death to be understood in a figurative sense, where the individual is conscious as he or she goes through a purging or refining process? I don't believe we can say definitively one way or the other from what the Bible tells us. But whichever is the case, the lake of fire will not be an enjoyable experience, and it should be avoided at all costs (by believing God).

We know the lake of fire will exist for the eons of the eons, but we are not told how long individuals will remain there. We have taken the liberty of assuming that some will only require a short time in the lake to be made ready for the kingdom, and these will experience "a dip in the lake." But others may require a longer stay, or a "swim in the lake."

"DISABLED LIST"
A period of time when a person is still alive but has not made a definite decision for the Lord. A time of "limbo".

ETERNAL
G. Morgan Campbell expressed it best, noting there is no word in the Greek that translates to our English word "eternal" and which means endless. When God is described as an "Eonian God" this does not mean He is not, in fact, eternal. It is just that the Bible talks about things as they exist or occur in this time period known as the eons. God is eonian, but He will also continue to exist after the eons are concluded.

"FIRST ROUND DRAFT CHOICE"
Based on the above notes concerning believers and non-believers, I use the phrase "first round draft choice" for believers ... those who believe by faith in this present age. I use this phrase because the believers will be the first to be resurrected. (See "Resurrection" a bit further down in this section.) I also like the phrase because most people reading this book will be familiar with draft choices because of college sports, especially the yearly draft of college football players. Who will be the number one draft choice is always a hot topic.

"GRADUATE"
When a person finally moves up from the "pit", or "lake of fire", after truly acknowledging Jesus as his/her Lord and Saviour. It may take a nanosecond or millions of years depending on the person's heart (pride, ego, arrogance, etc.).

HEAVEN

Sometimes the word heaven, or heavens, speaks of the atmosphere directly above the earth. Other times it speaks of somewhere well beyond, but its precise location is not revealed.

The Israelites never had any concept of "going to heaven." Their hope and expectation was the coming of the Messiah to establish His kingdom upon the earth. This is what Jesus speaks of during His earthly ministry. "Repent, for the kingdom is near." After His resurrection, when the apostles asked if this was the time He intended to restore the kingdom unto Israel, He did not tell them they had it all wrong. He simply said it was not theirs to know God's timing (Acts 1:6-7). Israel is God's instrument upon the earth. When He returns, born-again Israel will serve a purpose in Christ's reign. Today Israel, which rejected the Messiah, is temporarily set aside as Christ now draws those of the nations into the body of Christ. But this "stubbornness" in Israel is temporary (Romans 11:25-26). When the events described in Revelation take place, Israel will once again play a part.

Paul speaks of things not previously revealed, and one of those things is "heaven." Those of Israel look for Christ to come to earth, where their expectation lies in the ages to come. We within the body of Christ look for Christ to come and snatch us away to be with Him, where we will play a part in the heavens in the ages to come.

Sorry, but there are few details provided in the Bible. The notion of pearly gates and St. Peter admitting us are non-Biblical notions, not based on the Scriptures. The images we see in Revelation pertain to the earth; either this present earth or the new earth. The New Jerusalem with all of its splendor comes down out of heaven, but is not heaven itself.

Who goes to heaven? The body of Christ (believers) will be called up to meet the Lord in the air, and we will serve the Lord in the heavens (see the section below that speaks about the resurrection). When all things are reconciled to God and He becomes All in all (1 Corinthians 15:28), the entire universe will be under the realm of God's kingdom. It has not been revealed to us exactly what this will look like; who will be in heaven and who will be upon the new earth. Without details being provided, we will need to trust God as to the place He has planned for each of us. But He is our Heavenly Father, filled with grace and love, and most certainly we can trust Him for what lies ahead!

HELL

When we see this word in an English translation, it comes from one of three Greek words; Hades, Gehenna or Tartarus. Hades simply means "unseen." It is the temporary destination for everyone when they die, righteous and wicked alike. The flesh returns to the soil, the spirit returns to God, and the soul goes to "the unseen place" (Hades). The Hebrew "Sheol" in the Old Testament is the equivalent to "Hades" in the Greek. Bible translators have tainted the pure Word of God with their opinions and theologies. When they find Hades or Sheol with reference to one who is wicked, they translate it "hell." But when they find the same word with reference to one who is righteous, they translate it "grave" or "death." If we look at Hades and Sheol in every instance where they occur, we will see they simply refer to the unseen place where the soul goes immediately upon death. (See "What happens to us when we die" a bit further down.)

Gehenna refers to a physical location outside of Jerusalem; the Valley of Hinnom. Jesus makes reference to this place when He speaks of the disgraceful burial place for certain criminals executed in the age to come. But it is not a place where souls are cast "forever and ever" to be tormented.

Tartarus is a place where wicked spirits (demons) are imprisoned. No person is ever said to be cast into Tartarus.

INFERNO
See Dante's Inferno.

"LAKE OF FIRE"
This comes the closest to the common notions concerning hell, with two primary differences. First, the lake of fire does not last "forever and ever," but only for the eons of the eons (several eons, which we recall are periods of time with a beginning and an end). Second, the purpose of the lake of fire is not to torture and torment, but to bring about a positive conclusion in accord with God's plans.

Matthew may be alluding to the lake of fire when he tells of the judgment to come when Christ returns and judges those living upon the earth based upon their works (Matthew 25:31-46). In verse 46, those who do not pass the test are not cast into eternal torment, but will experience "eonian chastening." Even the well respected William Barclay indicated that the Greek words used in this instance are never used to imply destruction, but constructive chastening.

Revelation 20:15 tells us what the lake of fire is … "the second death." And in 1 Corinthians 15:27 we see that as all things are brought into subjection to Christ, the last enemy (death) is abolished. So there is a conclusion to the lake of fire.

"MOVED UP"
See "graduate".

"NON-BELIEVER"
A "non-believer" is one who does not believe. Doubting Thomas is a good example. Thomas knew what Jesus had said about His

upcoming resurrection, just like the other apostles did. Upon hearing the testimony of those returning from the empty tomb, the others believed. But not Thomas. He would not believe until he could see for himself, and touch Jesus. But did Jesus cast him away for his failure to believe? No. He allowed Thomas to see and touch Him.

Some will believe in this current lifetime, by faith. Others will not believe until they can see for themselves. But one way or the other, in this life or the next, there will come a day when every knee will bow before the Lord and all are reconciled to God the Father.

RELEASE

In professional baseball, a "release" is when a player gets let go, or fired, from a team or from an organization. In the context of this book, "release" means when a person dies physically, and can no longer make a decision for God while he is still physically alive.

"ROSTER"

"First round draft choices"—believers.

"SAVED"

This is an interesting word. If you were raised in the church, you'll immediately think you know what "saved" means ... that you are saved from eternal torment.

The word saved is used many times in the Bible. It sometimes means one's life is saved from being killed by an enemy. It sometimes means saved from disease (equivalent to being healed). Most often in the New Testament it means saved from the indignation or tribulation that we read about in Revelation.

The "believer" is saved from the second death, which is the fate of those who do not believe, and from experiencing the Great

Tribulation if it should begin in his lifetime. This is because the "believer" will be "snatched away" (raptured), or resurrected first. We will discuss this more a bit further down in the last section under "The Resurrection".

SECOND DEATH
See the Lake of Fire.

ST. AUGUSTINE
Augustine of Hippo is one of most well known church fathers. He died in 430 AD. Prior to Augustine there were a variety of beliefs on various subjects. Augustine set out to determine the correct (orthodox) position on these subjects. While many within the church believed God would ultimately save all mankind, Augustine worked to incorporate eternal torment (hell) into the orthodox belief system. Any who opposed eternal torment were deemed to be heretical. We must remember, however, that orthodoxy is an **opinion** concerning the various topics it addresses. It may, or may not be the truth. If Augustine (or others of the church fathers) were wrong on some points, it is difficult to escape the errors since most within the church will not question "orthodoxy." I believe (and many biblical scholars agree) that Augustine was totally wrong in his opinion of 'eternal' torment. Many of the Greek Church fathers understood that eonian did not mean endless, and that God would one day restore all mankind. Augustine was of the Latin strain and opposed the position.

"SWIM" IN THE LAKE
See "dip" in the lake (of fire).

TWO BILLION MAN ROSTER
Comprised of "first round draft choices" that aren't starters on the alleged "All Saints" team but are "on the team". Similar to all the

players on a sports team that don't happen to be "on the field" during a game but are "on the team", or, "on the bench" none-the-less. It is a term associated with the fictitious, 1,000 year millennial game to be played on earth during the millennium between God's team (All Saints) and the devil's team (Lucifer's Losers).

Consideration of Some Questions

WHAT HAPPENS TO US WHEN WE DIE?

The Greek philosophers have us convinced that our souls are immortal, but we are told that only Christ is immortal (1 Timothy 6:16). When we die our body returns to the soil, and our spirit returns to God Who gave it (Ecclesiastes 12:7). But our soul, which was generated when God animated the soil with His spirit, goes to an "unseen place." The word in Greek is "Hades," and in the Hebrew is "Sheol."

Convinced that we are immortal and that our soul must be accounted for, most Bible translators use "hell" for Hades if the passage is referring to one who is wicked, or "grave" if the passage is referring to one who is righteous. But the fact is that every person, righteous and wicked alike, go to Hades; the unseen place. Here we have no consciousness (see Ecclesiastes 9:5 and Psalm 6:5). This is why those who are dead are sometimes referred to as asleep, where we also have no consciousness. We are totally dependent upon God to resurrect us, as He has promised to do. At the time we are resurrected, we will "put on immortality" (1 Corinthians 15:53-54).

Some will object, pointing to passages such as Luke 23:43 when Jesus tells the thief on the cross beside Him, "I say to you, today you will be with Me in paradise." But all such passages are either mistranslated or misinterpreted, because the translator believes we are immortal and renders the translation with that bias. As for Luke 23:43, since there is no punctuation in the original Greek, the placement of the comma in this sentence is an interpretation. Based on what we know from elsewhere in the Scriptures about death, the passage should have been translated: "I say to you today, you will be with Me in paradise", not "today you will be with Me in paradise".

Others will object, saying: "Are you saying my loved one is not in heaven right now?" Personally I am comforted just as much knowing that my loved ones are asleep, and that the next conscious moment they will experience will be with the Lord. And furthermore, what becomes of us is not determined by our own wishes or desires, but by God Who created us and Who is in full control of our destinies.

THE RESURRECTION (WHAT LIES AHEAD?)
As the world conditions grow worse, we ask ourselves what lies ahead. How can God be in control, when all we read about in the newspaper is tragedy? Could it be that by allowing every government plan and program to fail, even when they have the best of intentions, we are learning of our total dependence upon God? We must realize that no person or governmental system can save us! With this in mind, let's consider what lies ahead, from what the Bible tells us.

THE RAPTURE -- Resurrection event #1 (1 Thessalonians 4:13-18): The dead in Christ will be raised, along with those in Christ who are alive, when "the rapture" occurs. This event is not told elsewhere in the Scriptures, but only by Paul who was given the "gospel of the Uncircumcision" (Galatians 2:7-9). Paul writes that those in Christ will be "snatched away" to meet the Lord in the air. This is a different event from when Christ returns to the earth to reign. Israel awaits His return to the earth, to restore the kingdom unto Israel (see Acts 1:6-7). But the body of Christ awaits Him to snatch us away to meet Him in the air. Israel's expectation is to serve God upon the earth when Christ reigns. Our expectation is to serve Him in the celestials (the heavens), where we will be a display of His grace in the oncoming eons (Ephesians 2:6-7).

After this resurrection of the body of Christ, the time of God's indignation (The Great Tribulation) as foretold in the book of Revelation will occur. Note that the body of Christ is to be rescued out of the coming indignation (1 Thessalonians 1:10). God did not appoint us to indignation (1 Thessalonians 5:8-9).

At the conclusion of this time of Tribulation, Christ will return to the earth (Revelation 19:11 and following).

Thrones will be setup, and there will be a judgment of those living at the time of Christ's return (Revelation 20:4 and Matthew 25:31).

Resurrection event #2 (Revelation 20:4-5): The passage refers to this event as "the former resurrection". Those who have been executed because of the testimony of Jesus and because of the word of God, and who do not worship the wild beast or its image, and who did not take the emblem (mark) of the beast will be resurrected. These will live and reign with Christ a thousand years (Revelation 20:5).

After the thousand year reign, Satan will be loosed (Revelation 20:7) and will deceive the nations, mobilizing them for battle.

The Adversary (Satan) will be cast into the lake of fire to be tormented for the eons of the eons (at least two eons, out of all the eons).

Resurrection event #3 (Revelation 20:11-15): The sea and Hades give up their dead. They are resurrected and stand before the throne and are judged in accord with their acts. Those not found in the scroll of life are cast into the lake of fire. (Note that the duration of their time in the lake of fire is not mentioned as it was for the Adversary.)

Then we see this present heaven and earth coming to an end, and the creation of a new heaven and a new earth (Revelation 21:1).

Some time after this, when all are subjected to God, will come the "consummation" (1 Corinthians 15:20-28). This is the climax of history. As in Adam all are dying, so also in Christ are all made alive. Christ reigns until all enemies are under His feet (subjected to Him), and the last enemy (death) is abolished. Christ is then subjected to God the Father, as God becomes All in all.

A WORD ABOUT BIBLE TRANSLATIONS

Today there are many different Bible translations to choose from. Many of the newer ones have been written for commercial purposes, so as to sell them and make a profit. And as translators try to make the Bible easier to read, they integrate more of their opinions and theologies into the translation, making them interpretations instead of translations. Many different Hebrew or Greek words may be translated using a single English word, making it impossible to recognize distinctions without using laborious study guides. The translators have done this because they have determined there is no practical difference between the various Hebrew and Greek words. What if they are wrong? Similarly, a single word in the Hebrew or Greek may be translated using many different English words with drastically different meanings. Here the translators assume to know that God was using a single word to refer to very different ideas. Could the translators be wrong in their assumptions?

I appreciate the Concordant Version, not because I trust the translators more than other translators, but because of the methodology used. Great care is taken to allow the reader to distinguish between different Greek or Hebrew words. Whenever possible, an English word is only used for a single Greek or Hebrew word, and each Hebrew or Greek word is translated using the same consistent English word or idea. There is a keyword concordance in the back of the New Testament that allows the reader to look at all other instances where the same Greek word was used, thereby checking the translation.

This methodology may make the translation more difficult to read, but it also preserves the distinctions made in God's Word in the original languages, and it prevents the bias of the translator from creeping into the translation as much as is humanly possible.

Recommended Resources

I have tried to provide just a brief overview of God's plan for mankind. As you study God's Word and think for yourself, I recommend the following resources as being useful along the way..

"At the End of the Ages" by Bob Evely. A basic but thorough overview of the biblical evidence showing God's plan to save all. Available by special order from most bookstores, or from www.GraceEvangel. org

"Christ Triumphant" by Thomas Allin. Reprinted by and available from www.concordant.org

"The Concordant Version" of the Bible. Concordant Publishing Concern from www.concordant.org

"Destined For Salvation" by Kalen Fristad. A great book planting seeds of hope of God's unlimited love and salvation. Available from www.universalistchristians.org

"God's Eonian Purpose" by Adlai Loudy. A more detailed consideration of God's plan to save all mankind. Available from www.concordant.org

"The Greek Word Aion-Aionios, Translated Everlasting-Eternal, in the Holy Bible, Shown To Denote Limited Duration" by John Wesley Hanson. Reprinted by and available from Saviour of All Fellowship, P O Box 314, Almont, MI 48003.

"Hope Beyond Hell" by Gerry Beauchemin. A book that builds a case affirming all God's judgments have a good and remedial purpose. Available from www.tentmaker.org

About the Author

Fritz Peterson was born Fred Ingels Peterson in Oak Park, Illinois on February 8, 1942. He grew up in a suburb of Chicago, Mt. Prospect, Illinois until he attended Northern Illinois University in 1960. Fritz earned his undergraduate degree in Physical Education in 1965, a Masters Degree in Education, 1967 and a Certificate of Advanced Study in Education (30 hours beyond a Masters) in 1973. He was also an instructor at Morehead State University in 1967 during the off season as well as at Northern Illinois University during off seasons from 1968 through 1971.

He was inducted into the NIU Hall of Fame in 1987 for his baseball accomplishments at NIU from 1961 through 1963 and with the New York Yankees from 1966 through 1974.

Fritz pitched in the 1970 All Star Game for the American League and won 20 games for the Yankees that year. He led the American League 5 years in a row in the fewest walks per inning pitched, a feat that was last accomplished by Cy Young in 1903.

Fritz is in the top 20 all time pitching leaders for the Yankees in several categories and ended up having the lowest ERA (earned run average) of ALL TIME in Yankee Stadium history (2.52 era). Whitey

Ford ranked 2nd (2.55 era). That record will never change hands since the original Yankee Stadium was replaced in 2009 by a new stadium.

Fritz was the starting pitcher in the last game Mickey Mantle homered in and was also the starting pitcher in the last game to be played in the original "House that Ruth Built" on September 30, 1973.

Peterson was involved in what Sports Illustrated called the most highly publicized trades in all of sports history when he and a Yankee teammate traded wives in 1973.

Fritz travels from New York to Colorado raising money for prostate cancer research for the University of Iowa Holden Comprehensive Cancer Center and writing books about the grace of God!

Bibliography

Allin, Thomas. "Christ Triumphant," Canyon County, CA: Concordant Publishing Concern, 1909. A real deep study into the history of God saving everyone, and how the "church" has covered up the teaching. Don't give this to your parish priest for Christmas.

Appel, Marty. "Now Pitching For the Yankees," Toronto, Canada: Sport Classic Books, 2001. Another fact filled and entertaining book from a former New York Yankee public relations man and successful sports author.

Balthasar, Hans Urs Von. "Dare We Hope 'That All Men Be Saved'," San Francisco: Ignatius Press, 1988. A Catholic priest delves into the scriptures and finds the "truth". Great reading for Catholics who have questions about grace from a priest's research on the subject. Of course, Hans was subsequently labeled a "heretic" by the church.

Beauchemin, Gerry. "Hope Beyond Hell, The Righteous Purpose of God's Judgment," Olmito, TX: Malta Press, 2007. Very good and detailed book about refuting an "endless hell". The book quotes Psalms 136: 1, that God's mercy endures forever, not thwarted by the grave. Shows how all God's judgments have a good and remedial purpose.

Brown, Steve. "When Your Rope Breaks," Grand Rapids, MI: Baker Books, 1988. A good book showing that God is in control and even uses Satan for his involvement in our lives for His good.

Corner, Daniel D. "The Believer's Conditional Security," Washington, PA: Evangelical Outreach, 2000. This book scared me into thinking that "once saved always saved" (OSAS) wasn't accurate. Although he did prove his point, I found that God's grace turned out ever better than OSAS. "All", rather than "some", will be saved sooner or later! Thanks Daniel for making me research further than I had planned. That research changed my life!

Evely, Robert W. "At The End of the Ages," Bloomington, IN: Authorhouse, 2003. One of the easiest reading, fact filled books available from a pastor and wonderful man who has become a great friend. It is a book with a thorough overview of the biblical evidence showing God's plan to save all.

Fristad, Kalen. "Destined For Salvation," Dows, IA: Kalen Fristad, Publisher, 2003-06. A great book planting seeds of the hope of God's unlimited love and salvation. A study guide is also available.

Gulley, Philip, and Mulholland, James. "If God Is Love," New York, NY: Harper Collins Publisher, Inc., 2004. An exciting book of hope but lacking some truths by insinuating that hell may not be real.

Gulley, Philip, and Mulholland, James. "If Grace is True," New York,

NY: Harper Collins Publishers, Inc., 2003. A great starter book that opens up grace to God's unending love. This is the book that started me on my exciting journey through God's unlimited grace. I overlooked some of the author's shortcomings due to the exciting main subject I had never thought about before; that God will save every person, in time.

Hanson, John Wesley. "The Greek Word Aion-Aionios, Translated Everlasting-Eternal, in the Holy Bible, Shown To Denote Limited Duration," Whitefish, MT: Kessinger Publishing Company, 2008. If anyone thinks there aren't many verses pointing to the salvation of all in the Bible, this is a good old book (written in 1878). It shows the reader the verses in both the old and the new testament.

Hitchcock, Mark. "55 Answers to Questions About Life After Death," Sisters, Oregon: Multnomah Publishers, 2005. An interesting book answering many questions people have about where people go after death. Not real specific when it comes to "the big one", what happens if a person ends up in hell.

Hitchens, Christopher. "God is Not Great: How Religion Poisons Everything," Lebanon, IN: Twelve Books, Hatchette Book Group, 2007. I laughed at the stuff "religion" has done to God. I would never have read something like this before 2006, but thoroughly enjoyed the book now. I could have added a few things to the book myself after having gone "around the block" with "religion" during my lifetime.

Lamott, Anne. "Bird by Bird: Some Instructions on Writing and Life," New York: Anchor Books, 1997. A book that real people can relate to. Single mom, struggling to raise her son, etc... Even uses the "f" word!

Lamott, Anne. "Traveling Mercies: Some Thoughts on Faith," New York: Anchor Books, 1999. More practical, life living stuff showing a regular person can have faith in God even if it is in a little different way than most.

Loudy, Adlai. "God's Eonian Purpose," Canyon County, CA: Concordant Publishing Concern, 1974. A more detailed consideration of God's plan to save all mankind.

Lucado, Max. "In The Grip of Grace," Nashville: W. Publishing Group, 1996. A nice book about grace, but actually limits God's grace to this side of the grave.

Lutzer, Erwin, W. "One Minute After You Die," Chicago: Moody Press, 1977. A book I used to rely on, especially when thinking about a person who just died. (At the time I believed Lutzer's conclusion, that's all I could think about, feeling very sad for folks having gone to hell, forever! It didn't seem right, and wasn't).

McDowell, Josh. "New Evidence That Demands a Verdict,", Nashville: Thomas Nelson Publishers, 1999. If one doubts the authenticity of the Bible, or Jesus, this is the book to read.

McVey, Steve. "Grace Walk", Eugene, Oregon: Harvest House Publishers, 1995. Very basic, good book about God creating us and who we are, not what we do.

Meyer, Joyce. "If Not For the Grace of God," New York: Warner Faith, 1995. Joyce is a great speaker and touches on why few pastors will preach on grace (pg. 174). Joyce, like most evangelists and preachers, won't tell the "rest of the story" about grace. Ask Carlton Pearson why.

Miller, Donald. "Blue Like Jazz," Nashville: Nelson Books, 2002. Anne LaMott's writings inspired Miller's book, and then another. Anne gave us permission to be human. Miller takes it to the college campus, showing faith another way that I could relate to from my college days. Explains why there's not much to read in the Christian marketplace unless it concerns self-righteousness and conservative propaganda.

Miller, Donald. "Searching For God Knows What," Nashville: Nelson Books, 2004. His second book goes a little deeper than his first one. He has inspired me to write for "real people" bearing our humanity once in a while. Miller drops a "four letter word" once in a while. His books are well written, funny, and carry a good message about God but don't go as far as I do into God's unlimited grace.

Pearson, Carlton. "The Gospel of Inclusion," New York, NY: Atria Books, 2006. Minister Pearson began preaching about universal reconciliation at his Tulsa, Oklahoma church, (Higher Dimensions), of over 5,000 members in the early 2000's and was promptly labeled a "heretic" by the Joint College of African-American Pentecostal Bishops in 2004. He lost his church and building through foreclosure in 2006 because of it. He is still preaching the salvation of all, labeling it the "Gospel of Inclusion" at a new location calling his new church, New Dimensions Church. His new church is growing!

Piper, Don. "90 Minutes in Heaven," Grand Rapids, MI: Fleming H. Revel, 2004. I got this book because it looked like fun to see what Heaven might be like. It's exciting. It would be even more exciting if everyone who reads this book would know that they were positively going to Heaven one day!

Piper, Don. "Heaven is Real," New York: The Berkley Publishing Group, 2007. A follow up book to his first. Not that meaningful of a book.

Russell, Bertrand. "Why I Am Not a Christian," New York, NY: A Touchstone Book, 1957. Like the Hitchens book, Russell lists things "religion" and "man" have done to make religion seem laughable at best, pathetic at worst. Both men are ('were' for Russell) very intelligent and site many of the idiotic things man does to man "in god's name". I feel bad for Russell since he's dead and will be getting a long "swim" in the "lake of fire". There's still time for Hitchens.

Talbott, Thomas. "The Inescapable Love of God," Boca Raton, FL: Universal Publishers, 1999. This book is "it". I want Professor Emeritus Talbott of Willamette University in Oregon to defend me in my belief in God's unlimited grace when I am accused of heresy by church people. This is a book to keep as a reference. Your pastor couldn't preach the same way again if he read this book.

Tolle, Eckhart. "A New Earth," New York, NY: Penguin Group, 2006. Oprah Winfrey put this book on the map and it is worth reading. Tolle is careful to not offend any religions and exposes inauthentic living in the process. Ego can play a negative roll in a person's life until it is exposed. Almost a cognitive therapy book.

Vincent, Ken R. "The Golden Thread," New York, NY: iUniverse, Inc., 2005. An easy reading book showing that God is the parent of all, and in the end will save the "lost sheep" and the "prodigal son".

Walsch, Neale Donald. "Home With God—In a Life That Never

Ends," New York, NY: Atria Books, 2006. A book that shows us that God is there forever whether we believe it or not. Take your choice.

Watson, David Lowes. "God Does Not Foreclose," Nashville: Abington Press, 1990. This book has so much it is hard to choose a high point. Bottom line, "The reality of our salvation is that Christ has accomplished it for us, (already), whenever we happen to accept it, and whether or not we happen to feel it or believe it at any given moment." (The quote is on page 109 of his book). (I added the 'already' to Watson's quote).

Weise, Bill. "23 Minutes in Hell," Lake Mary, Florida: Charisma House, 2006. I bought this book to see what Bill Wiese had to say. It was interesting but is way off talking about hell being everlasting. The truth is, sadly enough, that many people will experience hell after the Lord returns but nobody will be there "forever"! Who knows, maybe Mr. Wiese will take a "dip" himself?

Williams, Walter. "Love Without Limit," McAlisterville, PA: Probe Publishing Co. 2004. Walter Williams shows God's plan to save everyone by freeing them at the end from the evil that is in all of us. A very loving book from a minister of 50 years telling the whole story of the salvation of all.

Yancey, Philip. "What's So Amazing About Grace?" Grand Rapids, MI: Zondervan, 1997. Another tremendous book by Yancey, acclaimed by many as "one of the best books on grace ever written". Yancey mentions some of his shortcomings once in a while, as in his other books. I appreciate that. Maybe Phil will take "grace" all the way home in a future book of his.

Printed in the United States
153891LV00002B/17/P